AS THE FISH WHEEL TURNS

BY
PAULA CINIERO

Available as a digital ebook

ISBN 979-8-3045401-4-8 (Paperback)

ISBN 979-8-3050698-1-5 (Hardcover)

Publify Publishing

Lampasas, TX

contact@publifypublishing.com

Cover photo is courtesy of Allison Wild

TABLE OF CONTENTS

ACKNOWLEDGEMENTS

I really have a lot of people to thank. Not for this book as much as my life and experiences. I want to thank my parents for all they did for me. I also want to thank my partner Jim Knopke for being so supportive, never complaining about my traveling for work or for any other training that I have done.

There have been many people in my life that have had an influence on my learning and my adventures. Whether they know it or not, they have a place in this story. I want to thank them by listing them here, starting with those that are no longer on this earth plane. Clifford and Pauline Lanier, Nicola Ciniero and Maria Petteruti- (I never knew them but know that their DNA runs through me), Paul and Mary Starr, Sally Henry, Shirley M Moses, Dr. Rita Blumenstein - Traditional doctor, Lester Erhart, Joee Redington Jr., Richard and Shannon Hayden. Those that are still on this plane who have left me a different person and given my knowledge, I say Mahsii Cho, Gunalcheesh, Quyanna, Pinamaya, Ana Basee, Grazie, Thank you. Linda Johnson, Jonna Rae Bartges, Suellen Geis, Trimble and Mary Gilbert, Brenda Gilbert, Abraham Henry, Shirley Kruger, Sharon Demoski, Martina Ekada, Dr. Penny Burdick, Uttam Bajarcharya, Shanti and Ganga Bajracharya, Dr. Aihun Kuhn, Joan LaFauci Daniel Hayden, The Erhart Family, Cletus

& Remy (they did not want their names not mentioned), Laurie Thomas, Samson and Beverly Peter, Allen Tritt, Kimberly Andon (for letting me take off my cultural thinking cap and not being offended), Teresa Hicks, Kenny Smoker, Adeline Rose Smoker, Rose Atkinson, Robert White, Roger White Jr., Kim Ebey, Mike Owens, Kim and Harry Douglas, Corrine Lundell and Erin Meehan, Tami Jerue, Tia Holley, Debbie Dementieff, Naomi Michaelson, Estelle Thomson, Amelia Simeonoff, Elsie Boudreau, Roxanne Frank, Raven Cunningham, Phyllis D. Light, Amy Seifert, all of the students I have worked with in the Alaskan villages and the Fort Peck Reservation, and Amanda Armstrong at Publify Publishing who was willing to take a chance on this book.

DEDICATION

To Sammy who taught me more about dog mushing than any human and to Bubba who showed and taught me about unconditional love.

CHAPTER I

THE BEGINNING

I graduated from the University of Maryland School of Nursing with a Bachelor's Degree in Nursing. This was not my first career choice. In fact, it had never even been a thought. As I came into my teens, I so wanted to be an archeologist. My parents did not want me to be an archeologist, I remember my mom saying, "they don't make any money and your dad and I are paying for your education so you are not going to pursue that career". I was angry over not being able to do what I wanted to do but they were paying for my college education, at least for four years so what could I say? I was taught respect growing up and what your parents said was the law.

During my senior year of high school, I decided I wanted to be a physical therapist. That was okay with my parents. Of course, by then I had my whole life planned. I would be a physical therapist, move to North Carolina, get married and have children.

Wow, as I write this it even seems like a different person or a different lifetime.

I never did attend Physical Therapy school. I had a hard time with college physics and finite math, so my GPA was not high enough. I actually failed both classes the first time, lacking the insight to drop them early enough. So, I had to retake them anyway and passed both the second time. Just like today, 40 years ago getting into PT school was highly competitive. When I decided I just could not get there without retaking other classes to continually try and increase my grade point average, I started to look around at what else I could do. My parents kept saying…be a nurse…be a nurse. All I thought was I could never give a shot. HA!! Looking back over my career, I have given thousands of shots to children and adults.

I am very grateful to have become a nurse, because I could move anywhere and get a job. There were a lot of things I specialized in with nursing. However, working with different cultures was the most appealing and important aspect for me.

I worked in my own Southern culture (and it is its own culture!) in North Carolina and Kentucky, I worked in my Italian culture in New Jersey, I was also blessed to work in the Hispanic community in Kentucky and most of all within the Alaska Native community and the Assiniboine/Sioux community on the Fort Peck Indian reservation.

No matter how much we try and plan our life, there is already a plan I think that we are entirely unaware of and it plays itself out in very interesting ways, putting obstacles, people, experiences in our life that are there to teach us.

So here is my story:

I moved to North Carolina after graduating nursing school and got my first job at Duke University Medical Center on the GI surgery unit. I did get married when I was in North Carolina and we moved to New Jersey and then to Washington State. I decided at that time I did not want to be married anymore. I think it was just the thing that had been expected of me and my generation at that time. Also, all of my friends were getting married. Brian was a great person but not the right one for me. When I left him, I moved in with a long-time co-worker and friend. We were both working for a home health agency in Seattle. I was working with AIDS patients giving investigational drugs at home. This was in the middle 1980s when HIV/AIDS hit the US wreaking havoc on the gay male population. It was a learning and a growth time for me. It was an awesome nursing experience and one that I have not seen repeated anytime since then. At that time there was only one FDA approved drug for HIV and really none that were approved for any of the AIDS related complexes. It was a time that the FDA was approving compassionate use drugs for many of the AIDS diseases such as pneumocystis carinii pneumonia, CMV retinitis and mycobacterium avium tuberculosis. It was also a very hard time because all of my patients did die. It was very hard for their families because being a homosexual male in the 80s was not very accepted and when most of my patients started suffering with AIDS and knew they were going to die, they had to tell that to their

3

parents plus also come out to them at the same time. I remember that contrary to what we were taught in nursing school we encouraged our AIDS patients to smoke marijuana. It was the only thing that helped with pain and would in some cases increase their appetite. The only FDA approved drug AZT (azidothymidine/Zidovudine) was extremely expensive. Most insurances did not pay for it and I don't think Medicaid paid for it. Therefore, many of my patients could not afford it. If someone was taking it and died, the remaining AZT went underground to someone else they knew. It was very sad that the drug that could have helped in the early stages was so out of reach for most of the population and so the disease progressed very fast. It also progressed because it was not caught early enough and most medical providers did not know what was going on. It was a pivotal time for me as a person and a nurse. I was brought up Christian and was taught from a very young age that being homosexual was a bad thing and that they would go to hell. (I was also brought up that palm readers and spiritual advisors were all a hoax and out there to take your money). I did have a cousin who was gay. I remember trying to talk to my grandmother about it and she would vehemently deny that he had an alternative lifestyle. I really had to think about what **MY** feeling really was in regard to the homosexual population in terms of my job. After thinking about it, I concluded that I had no real thought one way or the other. To me, the population I was working with were sick and dying and that was all that mattered. I became very attached to a few, especially Patrick. He and his partner gifted me with a heart shaped basket when I left my job and it still has a place on my wall 36 years later. He died the day after I had left.

Even though I was loving my job, I did not have a home. Living with JZ was great and I will always be grateful for her taking me in at that time but something was missing. On one occasion, while doing some work at Harborview Medical Center, I was talking with a medical resident about how he would go to Alaska in the summer and work on fishing boats, making $60,000 in a summer.

That was not appealing to me but it made me start thinking about Alaska. It had never been a dream of mine to move there. Growing up in Maryland, all we learned about Alaska is that it was up there somewhere and that it snowed all the time.

For some reason after talking with that resident, I started doing more thinking about Alaska. Well actually, I think it may have started when my husband, at the time, and I moved to North Bend from Issaquah Washington. Our neighbors had a satellite dish and were able to get an Alaska TV station. (RATNET it was called then for those of you from AK). I remember one night we were over there and the coverage of the Iditarod Trail Sled Dog Race came on. I was fascinated by the dog teams and the terrain. So, I would go over every night at a certain time to watch the coverage the whole three weeks plus of the race. This watching of the Iditarod was a foreshadowing event in my life but I did not know it then. My husband and I separated shortly after that. While living with JZ, I also subscribed to the Fairbanks News Miner Sunday edition. I thought, let me look at the job listings and see what there is. Well… by week three, I had found a job that looked interesting.

It read:

Itinerant Public Health nurse to work out of Nome and travel to

Eskimo villages

Contact Norton Sound Health Corporation.

I did.

I quickly typed up a resume and sent it with a cover letter. I got a call. An interview was scheduled with the Nurse Manager for the public health department. She was of Italian descent and from Washington D C; 2 home runs for me. I was hired over the phone and was sent a plane ticket. Wow, that was so easy. So, I packed my snowsuit, boots, food, some clothes and off I went. I had a cute baby blue snowsuit. I was a skier so, of course, I had cool skiing clothes. I know my mother was disappointed and really had no idea why I was going to Alaska. My dad had died a year and a half before. I always wondered what he would have thought. It was February 1991.

CHAPTER 2

ALASKA THE FIRST TIME

I don't remember the flight from Seattle to Anchorage but I do remember the flight from Anchorage to Nome. The Alaska Airlines jet that travels that route is a full-size jet but only has roughly 18 rows. What is in between the pilot and passengers is freight. Now mind you this freight could be one or multiple teams of sled dogs, the food for the stores in Nome or surrounding villages, coffins of people who have passed away and are being taken home for burial or a variety of other things that are making their way to a remote village and being transitioned to a smaller aircraft in Nome. It was kind of crazy to see people coming on with bags from McDonalds. There is no McDonalds in Nome. Some people even had a particular smell about them. (as I later learned it was the smell of seal) And of course, I was actually seeing real live Eskimos for the first time in my life.

Looking back on that flight makes me laugh. I distinctly remember the pilot coming on the radio and saying" if you look off to your right you will see the village of McGrath". I looked out of the window and said to myself "Where?" All I saw was white. It was February in the Arctic. As we got farther north to Nome, I noticed there were no trees. It was all tundra. I had grown up around trees so this was going to be all new. Think of the Great Plains buried under a blanket of snow and you have the Arctic.

I know when I got off the airplane I really stood out in my baby blue snowsuit. Unknown to me at the time, there was a man there who frequented the airport in order to check out the new single nurses getting off the plane. I am sure it was easy for him to pick me out of the crowd. He eventually became a good friend and someone who was part of a pivotal point in my life. Nome and Bethel are both places that get a lot of nurses coming and going. During my time in Alaska, I would sometimes ask the other nurses where they went when they first came to Alaska and it was always one of those two places. They are very remote; it is hard to get consistent staff and the only way out is by airplane.

I was picked up at the airport by my new boss who had also arranged housing for me in Nome living with three other girls. Rita, Betsy and Marilee. Rita eventually moved back to her home state of Minnesota but I know Betsy and Marilee are still in Nome. They accepted me right away which is par for the course in Nome. It was an exciting place for me. There were a lot of people in their 20s and early 30s. There is a radio station KNOM that operates in Nome and is run by the Jesuits. A lot of young people came to Nome after college to volunteer at the radio station for a year or two. Most fell in love with Nome and stayed either for a long time or they left and came back finding they did not like life outside compared to Nome. I decided I wanted to have a dog and could not have one in the apartment I was staying in with the girls so I moved out into half of a duplex. I had to keep the dog outside but I really wanted one. He was a wolf hybrid named Kiowa. He lived to be 16 and lived in three different states with me before he died.

My neighbors then were Mike and Pat. Mike was an Iditarod veteran and was a wealth of information about the race. March is Iditarod time and Nome is the finish. Having come in February, I was just in time to see the race. Public health had a table with vaccine information at the race headquarters in Nome. I was manning the table one day and Mike who was a paramedic for Norton Sound Health Corp was at the table next to me. Sitting next to him was a very handsome Eskimo gentleman and they were visiting. Mike introduced me and the Eskimo man got a big smile on his face, a twinkle in his dark eyes and looked at me and said, " I am a REAL Eskimo". His name was Herbie Nayokpuk, the "Shishmaref Cannonball," a name given to him during the Iditarod. He had run many Iditarods in the beginning years of the race.

CHAPTER 3

THE JOB

At work I had a two-week orientation of reading manuals, you know, really exciting work, then I got to travel. My boss went with me several times just to do the village orientation and I was lucky I got to go to some of the villages she covered. I eventually went to all the villages in the Norton Sound region except for Little Diomede, which is a village on a tiny island. Yes, you can see Russia from there. I wish I had been able to go. It is a village on a rocky cliff, the weather can go down really fast and you could be stuck there for 1-2 weeks. Planes are very infrequent.

After those couple of trips with my boss, she let me loose by myself. This is something that seems to be present in Native health in the Bush, sink or swim, figure it out. I was cool with that although at times a little nervous going into a new village by myself.

I had witnessed a lot of drunk people in Nome. They were at times a little scary. I never wondered why there were so many in Nome. In the villages I never really noticed. I think it was because I was so wide eyed and new and I had only been a nurse 7 years by this time and besides the health aide I was the only medical care in the village. I guess I never thought about why there were so many Natives that were hard core drinkers. I don't think that entire period I was in the Region, I gave it much thought. I have since developed an understanding of this and will leave the explanation for later.

In those years of the early 1990s, when I would go to Savoonga and Gamble, the only two remaining villages on St. Lawrence Island (an island off the western coast of Alaska) I usually had to have someone interpret for me when I was seeing an elder or a preschool child. At that time English was not the first language and children did not learn it until they went to school. This made it difficult when we had to work a tuberculosis (TB) outbreak and try to teach people how to take their medicine. The Siberian Yu'pik language is the language spoken on the island. It was intriguing to listen to the language and hear people in the waiting room speak it. People there were also still living a mostly subsistence lifestyle including using sealskin to make their sled dog harnesses.

I remember on one of my trips to Savoonga, there were several polar bear hides hanging in the village. When I questioned someone about it they told me that there was a polar bear patrol that would patrol a 5-mile perimeter of the village and kill any polar bear within that perimeter. Children would always play outside unsupervised and polar bears are stealth. They can come grab a human, carry him off and his companion would never know it. Most of the villages around that region did polar bear patrols. In the village of Gambell, I went for a walk one evening after I closed the clinic. I walked up the hill behind the village. On one side of the hill was the village cemetery. I got to the top of the hill and the view was awesome over the village and onto the Bering Sea. The next day someone came in and asked me if that was me that had been climbing that hill and they proceeded to slightly admonish me for doing that alone because of the threat of polar bears wandering around.

Often, after the clinic would close for the day I would go walk around the villages. I remember the same trip to Gambell some children saw me walking. One of the children was from Russia and was visiting the village. She walked along the beach and would bend down and show me certain sea plants that had washed up on the shore and then she would show me how she ate them and then would have me try them. The children were always great. One one visit to Shishmaref, I went walking around. It was cold enough for me to have a coat on. The children saw me and followed me around like I was the pied piper (this happened all the time in all the villages). We got to the local swimming hole, where I saw bathing suits just lying on the ground. Some of the children just stripped off their clothes and put on those bathing suits and hopped in that swimming hole, which wasn't too large or deep. They would play for a while then get out and put their clothes on, all the while I was standing there watching them with my coat on just amazed they were not cold.

It was in the village of Savoonga that I really formed my admiration for Community Health Aides (CHA). They are the front-line health workers in the remote villages in Alaska. They evolved from the elder midwives, who delivered babies and knew the plant medicine, into a very structured, knowledgeable health care worker. The program officially started in the 1980s, but women had been working in that capacity for a long time.

The education needed to apply for a health aide position is a high school diploma/GED. The applicant is then sent to a series of 3–4-week classes. For a total of 4 sessions then they could apply to become a Community Health Practitioner (CHP). In Savoonga there was a CHP named Karen. I will never forget when someone came into the clinic to see her with his index finger cut half off, just hanging by some skin, and Karen saying to me "do you want to suture it?" I of course in my nurse way said I would like to watch her do it. We were never trained to suture in nursing school but here was a high school grad with 16 weeks of training doing the suturing. Of course, most Native women at that time knew how to sew skin for clothes, fur hats and fur ruffs so it was not a big stretch for them to learn how to suture. CHAs are taught how to suture, deliver babies, put in IVs and they also used to be able to give controlled substances, like morphine, by injection. That has been stopped due to the number of clinic break-ins to steal the controlled substances. Other than being amazed at what the health aides did, I never really thought about what the job was like for them until many years later when I was working in the villages in the Interior. These CHA providers have to take care of family members who are ill, dying, in traumatic snowmobile accidents and be able to keep it together while doing so.

While working in Nome, I worked for the Norton Sound Regional Health Corporation. Now the Public Health nurses that work in Nome are employees for the State of Alaska. The communities I serviced were Wales, Brevig Mission, Elim, Koyuk, Unalakleet, Stebbins and St. Michael. The villages are all Eskimo, but they are Inupiaq and Yup'ik. I was still shy then so I did not participate in the communities as much as I would have if I was there now. I did attend some dances where traditional dancing and drumming were done. I also really did not visit anyone, which to this day, I do regret because there were some fantastic elders alive then. I did have the pleasure of visiting one an elder in Wales a few times. Her name was Katie Tokienna. She did not speak any English so her son would come and translate for me. The only two words I think she did know in English were "epidemic flu". She would have been alive during that time of the "Great Death" but not very old. I wish I could have had more of her knowledge. Her son also told me a story about the old medicine woman, who was not a good one, but who lived in a cave on the hill by the village. At the time I was there, I was told that there were still some polar bear skulls marking where her place had been and that people had seen a seal flying on fire to that place. Whether that was her as a shape shifter I am not sure. I was also told never to go up to that place.

On one side of the village, there is a hill that faces Russia. One day, I decided to climb it because I thought it was cool to see Russian territory. There was a large metal sculpted outstretched hand about halfway up facing toward Russia, symbolizing peace, and several cairns at the top. I was told that the cairns at the top of the hill were put there a long time ago so that any warring people from Russia would see them and be deceived into thinking there were more people living in the village than there were or that people were on the hill waiting to kill intruders.

On that same hill about a quarter of the way up there was a burial ground and I remember walking around there; the markers were not there and there were some caskets that were open and had bones in them. I do remember one vividly that had the rusted butt of a rifle. I guess in those days' possessions were buried with the person. All of the villages in Norton Sound are on the water and most of the subsistence food came from the sea. It was not unusual to see ducks hanging on a rack outside, seal meat, walrus meat and whale meat all on drying racks.

In the winter, it was also not unusual to see washed clothes drying outside. They would hang them on racks. Because of the low humidity in Alaska, they would freeze dry- and then be brought in to warm by the fire.

All houses in those villages had an arctic entry way. In the Inupiaq language it is a qanisaq (pronounced kunny suck or kunny chuck depending on where you are in the region.) Those are wonderful places because when it is cold and windy you are not opening your door right into the main house and letting all the cold air in and the precious heat out. There were also a few houses where a ladder led to an opening in the top of the house and then another ladder led into the house. In Wales, and in a lot of the villages, the honey bucket was in the arctic entryway so it would not stink up the house. The houses all had wood stoves and were kept extremely warm. Even in Norton Sound, which is tundra and had no trees, people would collect driftwood to heat their homes. These windblown western coastal villages were at the mercy of the weather. In the village of Wales, it was not unusual to have snow drifts as tall as houses. Travelling could often be a struggle because of having to scale the enormous drifts.

At that time, all villages, and many now, still have no running water to the houses. The US Public Health service came to all the villages many years ago and installed washeterias. Washeterias are buildings where residents could get water, do laundry and take showers. Some villages now have running water. However, when I was working as an itinerant Public Health Nurse, there was at least one village in every region of the state I worked in that did not even have running water in the clinic!!! We would have to boil water and wash our hands in a pan. That was before they even invented hand sanitizer.

I was first introduced how to listen to and speak to a native culture while working in the Norton Sound region. Eskimos did not answer yes and no with words but with their eyebrows, so you had to really be paying attention. It took me a while to figure that out. I must have really seemed like an ignorant "kass'aq"(Yu'pik term for white person). Growing up in a non-Native culture that is loud, talking over one another, and expecting an immediate answer to a question, it is a hard thing to learn to watch and be still. It took some time to realize that those people were answering me even when there were no words exchanged. Also, older Natives at that time would not look at you when you spoke to them or they spoke to you because in their culture it is a sign of disrespect. I still see this in elders in the Alaska Native culture and with some on the Fort Peck Reservation.

In our fast, busy world we think we need to talk fast, get our answers and have the conversation over but that also did and does not happen in the Native communities. When asked a question, there may be a long pause, probably only about 5-10 seconds, (although it feels like minutes) when the person is taking their time thinking about how they are going to answer you. This has been extremely hard for non-Native nurses to understand and to deal with. Nurses also think that what they say as far as health teaching is the law and don't take into consideration what is relevant for the culture. I have found that you have to get the person's story and find out a little about their lives before you can really do any health teaching. It is amazing how many health care professionals working in

Native communities, even in the Lower 48, have no idea what is available in the community.

Time in the Native communities is also relative.

I will never forget the first time I went to the World Eskimo and Indian Olympics (WEIO). It was years later when I was living in Fairbanks. I was sitting in front of a few elder women I knew and the talk started about how late it was and the events had not started yet. I arrived an hour late and yet we were still waiting for another hour.. Finally, one of the elders said, "HMM, they must be running on Eskimo time. Indian time is only an hour late"!!!!

If you think about it, a long time ago, for most cultures time was unimportant. You did not have to be at a job by 8 am. The rest of the world is now focused on time but the subsistent cultures in Alaska don't worry about clock time but season time. Nowadays, people have jobs and have to get work on time but many people who live in the Bush still don't have regular jobs and do not need to worry about time as much.

Nome was a fun place to be. 9 bars and 9 churches. The bars are where you hung out even if you did not drink. There were a lot of people in my age group in Nome so I made some great friends. We all just had a great time. In the winter the girls I lived with would have people over for a potluck and we would all eat and play cards, which is a regular winter Arctic pastime.

I remember the first date I went on in Nome, we went to the dump. I know you are laughing but for a lot of people in villages it is a great first date, because a lot of times you can see bears at the dump!. I also had a guy take me on a date to look for the little men on the tundra. I cannot remember how to spell the Inupiaq name for them. But the best dates were going up to the White Alice site or the road leading to it and looking at the Northern Lights. It was there that I first heard them. Yes. They do have a sound. In Alaska you cannot see as many stars at night as you can in Montana or Wyoming but we do have the best Northern Lights. They " curtain", a movement like a wave, and they change colors. A lot of Northern Native cultures believe that the lights are the souls of the dead. Also, if the dogs bark at the lights, it is said, they are seeing their dead companions.

I have seen the most diverse colors of lights when outside of Fairbanks, the pink, purple, green all at the same time. When the lights are bright one can travel through the land without a headlamp or flashlight. That is the same when there is a full moon and snow on the ground. The moon reflects off the snow and you can go for a walk at midnight with no extra light. My time in Nome was rich and fulfilling. The only thing that I wish I would have done differently was to be more outgoing. There were still "Medicine Men" living in some of the villages. What an experience it would have been if I had been brave enough to go visit.

For my whole Public Health Nursing career, I have had to fly to work. At least to most of the villages where I worked. In the Nome region it was interesting to see who or what picked you up at the little airstrip when you arrived by bush plane. Each Bush airline has an agent in the village. An Agent is someone who picks up the mail from the post office and delivers it to the plane and vice versa, they haul freight and pick up and deliver passengers. Sometimes it was a vehicle, but back in the 90's it was either a 4-wheeler with a wagon for supplies, or a dog team or a snow machine with a sled on the back and you rode the runners of the sled with your gear in the sled. One time it was a dog team and sled. In the early days of Public Health nursing, you had to just about carry the entire clinic with you. I would very often have 9-10 bags of gear with me which included clinic supplies, my own food, clothes and my sleeping bag and sleeping pad. It was rare in the 90s that the clinics had sleeping quarters for the travelers. Most of the time I was sleeping on the floor. I will never forget on one trip to Wales, the clinic there was shaped like an igloo and for some reason that trip the clinic was cold. The traveling environmental health person was there as well and at night we slept right up against each other, just to keep warm. He and I did a lot of talking that night because even right against each other it was still too cold to sleep.

Wales was the coldest village I ever went to. I remember one winter day, I was spending the night at the home of a teacher (who did eventually become my fiancé but we never married) and the wind started to howl. I was leaving for the school, where I had to do some work and he told me to take his goggles and winter anorak to wear over my coat. He said I should not let any part of my skin be exposed because it would automatically become frostbitten. The wind chill that day was 90 degrees BELOW ZERO. The wind in that village also created large berms so it was like climbing mountains to get over the berms to the school.

I was introduced to dog mushing in Nome. A friend Mike (who was actually the man I mentioned earlier who came to the airport to check out all the single nurses arriving on the plane), was a dog handler for an Iditarod musher named Matt Desalarnos. One day Mike took me on my first dog sled ride. We flipped the sled and I bruised my arm really badly but I was hooked. It was soooo cool.

CHAPTER 4

IDITAROD TIME IN NOME

Iditarod, the 1000-mile dog sled race across Alaska. It commemorates the 1925 serum run to Nome from Nenana. There was a diphtheria epidemic in Nome and no vaccine anywhere in Nome. Children were getting very ill. Serum was delivered by train from Anchorage to Nenana, where teams of dogs in relay fashion took the lifesaving serum to Nome. The end of the Iditarod ,which starts the first Saturday in March, is in Nome. It is pretty much one big party, that is not to say it is a drunken party for that time but it is a party. All the bars have something going on while Nome waits for the mushers. When I was living in Nome there were wet T-shirt contests, bands playing, condom parties (where condoms were given as prizes) . Each bar had its own entertainment. There was even a golf event. Now picture this: you are going to play golf on the frozen Bering Sea. It is winter, and golf balls are white. There was a solution.. fluorescent orange golf balls, artificial turf around the hole. It was great fun to watch and oh we had a national forest as well on the ice. People saved their Christmas trees and they were put on the ice with wooden cutouts of animals and viola, The Nome National Forest.

There was an Iditarod race headquarters at the little convention center in Nome, where you could go in and get an update where the mushers were. When they were getting close, that means when they left the Safety Roadhouse, 22 miles from Nome, people would start to gather at the bars because they were all downtown and the race finish was on Main Street. When the musher is a mile from the finish the fire siren goes off and the masses of people pour out of the bars with their parkas, mukluks and other winter gear on and stand there and wait, no matter if there is a blizzard or it is dead calm. "Nomeites" just don't come out for the first musher but for everyone. It is such a celebration. There is a banquet held three days after the first musher makes it to Nome. In the 90's there were usually less than 50% of the mushers in Nome by that time, so Nome had a second banquet and a third banquet so that all mushers could be recognized. In the 90's it took almost three weeks for all the mushers to make it to the finish line. To my knowledge they do not have three banquets anymore. The race is much faster now so they don't need to.

I volunteered for the race that March and was sent out to the Safety roadhouse checkpoint. 22 miles from Nome it was the last checkpoint before the finish line. The mushers did not have to stay there but had to check in, have their mandatory gear checked and could stop and feed dogs and themselves. Safety roadhouse checkpoint was a bar. It was on the trail from Nome to White Mountain and the old community of Solomon was not far from there as well, so people would stop even when it was not during the race. I was able to check in mushers and help move dogs and drop bags. If a musher "dropped" a dog (leave a dog at a checkpoint), I would take care of the dog until it could be taken to Nome. We did not have a veterinarian at that checkpoint like all of the others. Even though there was a bartender there who always had some food going for mushers I would stay up 24 hours gazing into the complete blackness looking for the twinkle of a headlamp signaling a musher was coming. In the blackness you could see a headlamp miles away. Sometimes it felt like forever before they actually showed up. We also had a ham radio operator there that would announce to Nome who was coming through Safety. I was enamored with the dogs and the whole idea. It was surreal several years later when I stopped at that checkpoint with a team of dogs.

On subsequent visits when I would work for a month at a time, I would always try to go during Iditarod time and I would always volunteer with the race. The year I volunteered at the headquarters, I was asked to go help mark the trail from Topkok Hills to Nome. I borrowed a snow machine and sled and the three of us started out. We made it to Topkok and noticed the tripod markers were all down due to wind. That area is notorious for wind and just about the time we were setting up tripods again it started roaring with wind. We got those big markers right and then started our way back to Nome. The person in front of me had a drill with a router bit and drilled holes in the ice and hard packed snow and I placed the lathes in the holes. We did this from Topkok to Safety Roadhouse and a bit farther, then the trail was on the road and that had been marked. Somewhere between 3-5 miles from Nome, it was a total whiteout. I could not tell where the ground or the sky was and could not see more than 5 feet in front of me. I was not a proficient snow machine driver so I think I slowed down to 10 miles an hour. One of the guys I was with came back to check on me. Sad thing was I did not see him until he was almost on top of me.

The job as Itinerant Public Health nurse was one of the best jobs I ever had. I went to the remote areas and I was the only medical personnel, besides the CHA. There was always a doctor I could call in a hub community like Nome or Fairbanks. I got to do the stuff I needed to do but then was autonomous enough to do whatever else I thought needed to be done. That may include health teaching in the schools, doing elder home visits, taking stitches out of dogs Whatever it was I got to think and work outside the box.

I worked for Norton Sound for 6 months full time and then I moved back out of Alaska. My grandparents were not doing well and I wanted to be closer to them. So, I moved to Kentucky. I had a friend there and they encouraged me to try out living there. Fortunately for me, Norton Sound was always short of PHNs so they would hire me on a month at a time basis to go back to Nome and travel to the villages. I did this for three more years on and off. It was awesome to be able to go back. When I moved to Kentucky I came with two dogs, one was my wolf hybrid and one a retired sled dog that was from a Libby Riddles line. (Libby Riddles was the first woman to win the 1000-mile Iditarod Trail Sled Dog Race).

Paula skinning a Moose

Dogs and Tetons on
the Rocky Mountain
Stage Stop Trail

Life of a dog handler.
Handling for my friend
Gwen Bogart at the
Stage Stop Race

CHAPTER 5

ALASKA AGAIN

After I moved to Kentucky with my two dogs, my thoughts were still in Alaska. I had two harnesses for my dogs so I would tie them with a section of gangline to my ten-speed bike and have them pull me down the roads. It was an adventure on a 10 speed. I would never recommend that to anyone. I crossed some major roads with them and, of course, became a local celebrity. Well, those two dogs got together and I had an accidental litter of puppies. Of course, I kept all the ones that survived. I moved to a farm and rented that house where I had room for my expanding Southern team of dogs. A neighbor helped me build a wheeled rig so I could drive the dogs on the farm and on the roads and in parades. I remember calling Gareth Wright in those years I was in Kentucky to see if I could buy a leader, but he charged too much for me. I did end up buying a good leader from Jeff King, Sammy was his name. He was an awesome dog. Sammy taught me more about dog mushing than any person. During my years as a checker, I had met many dog mushers and I had kept in touch, after moving, with Dan MacEachen. We talked just about every week. I finally decided that I wanted to run the Iditarod. He and I talked about it and he told me that I could lease a team from him. We never did discuss price at that time, not the smartest move on my part. I planned to run and that is all I thought about. So, in 1994, I made plans to ship all the dogs to Alaska, with the exception of my Norwegian Elkhound "Munch". I took all my stuff back to my mother's house in Maryland and headed off to Alaska. My Uncle Joe met me somewhere along the way, it has been so long I do not remember, and he drove with me to Seattle. In Seattle, I met up with my friend Jennette (JZ) and she boarded the Alaska ferry with me headed for Haines, Alaska. My dog Munch had to stay in the truck the whole trip. JZ and I were saving money and did not get staterooms so we stayed on the deck in lounge chairs under heat lamps. Thank goodness for those heat lamps. The weather between Seattle and Southeast Alaska and all throughout Southeast Alaska is very rainy and cold but extremely beautiful. JZ departed the ferry when we landed in Juneau and headed back to Seattle. On board we met a Thunderbirds pilot who was heading up to Eielson Air Force base. He and I traveled together when we got off the ferry all the way to the Tok Junction split in Alaska. I was going to Anchorage to visit a friend before heading to Fairbanks. It was nice to have company on that trip along the highway.

I arrived at Dan MacEachen's house in Two Rivers, about 1.5 miles from where I now currently live. They were expecting me since my dogs had arrived 2 weeks before but they were surprised when the airport called them that my dogs were there. I guess maybe my plans had not been very clear. Dan was just building his house and the bedroom sleeping arrangements were a little odd. Dan had brought workers from Colorado up to work on the house and take care of dogs and I was the only woman. I decided to pitch a tent next to where my dogs were and I stayed in the tent until it started snowing at the end of September. By then Dan had hired a dog handler named Diane from Australia so I moved into the house and the three of us shared a bedroom. Dan did not want me ever to train his dogs by myself so he had me ride with Kathy Swenson all the time. He did toward the end allow me to take them out by myself and wouldn't you know it I got the 4-wheeler stuck in the muddy bog. The dogs would not pull it out for me. When I did not show up in a reasonable time someone came looking for me and they were able to get the dogs to pull the 4-wheeler out of the bog. After a while Dan and I talked about logistics. He wanted $30,000 for me to lease the team and I would have to sign an agreement that if any dog was injured, I would have to pay him the price of the dog and any vet fees. I did not think that was fair. I was pretty upset. I was still trying to decide what to do when I received a letter from Remy (not their real name). She and I had become friends at a previous Iditarod when I was a volunteer and I had kept in touch with their handler they had the year before. I had written to him and told him of my woes and he had passed it on. The letter I got from Remy stated that they were looking for a handler and if I wanted I could come down there and work for them with the dogs and possibly run a second team for them at no charge to me. The sigh of relief was tremendous. I, of course, wrote her back and we settled on the arrangements. They had a friend from Manley , Stephanie, who was coming to Fairbanks and she would meet me and I would follow her to Manley where Cletus (not his real name) and Remy would pick me and my dogs up by boat and we would go to their homestead which was on a slough of the Tanana river.

I remember going up the Elliott Highway and that at that time it was mostly gravel. When we arrived, I remember going to the boat landing and there were Cletus and Remy. We loaded my dogs from the truck to the boat, snapping their collars onto a chain that was run through the gunwales on the boat. There was a couple in the truck watching us as we were doing this. I asked Remy who they were and it was Freddy and Ada Jordan. Freddy wanted to see what kind of dogs I was bringing. Freddy had been a well-known dog musher in his time.

At that time, the Cletus & Remy had about 100 dogs. They had a big cabin, a smaller handler cabin, cache and an outhouse. The cabin was between the young dogs and the older dogs. I was to do most of the care, feeding and cleaning poop of the younger dogs and Cletus would take care of the race team. Plus, I had 13 of my own dogs at that time. The handler cabin was small. It had a table, a wood heat stove and a wood cook stove. The mattress was up in a small loft that was just a little bit bigger than the mattress and only high enough to crawl into. There was a homemade ladder that was used to get up into the loft. At the homestead there was no electricity, running water, phone or snow machine. There was a four-wheeler but everything else was done with dog power.

My life there was an experience I will never forget.

That year, not long after I arrived, the ice started to run. That means small patches of ice come down the river getting bigger and bigger and jamming together until the whole river freezes. It does not freeze smooth but in a jumble of ice chunks that are huge. If you measured the size of some of them they could be several stories high counting the part that is under the water. That year it took about a month from the time we saw the first chunks of ice until the river and slough were completely frozen. When the ice started to run we had to run. It was time to get the fall stuff done such as putting the fish wheel back, winching the boats up the bank out of the water. The day that Cletus and Remy decided to move the fish wheel they had used to catch dogfish, they left me at home and asked me to pull the "stink fish "out of the barrels.

Let me explain some of the terms in the last sentence. First, a fish wheel is a big wooden contraption with two extremely large baskets that turn and scoop fish out of the water into a box. (see picture on the front cover). It is made mostly out of wood and if left in the water during the winter will be damaged either in freeze up or break up. A lot of people actually haul theirs out of the water but some put them up a creek so they don't get slammed by the ice. That year that is what Remy and Cletus were doing. Second - stink fish- A delicacy among Alaska Natives but often used for dog food and a delicacy for dogs. They had a 50-gallon drum that was filled with fish topped with rocks and then the lid with rocks on the lid. While Remy & Cletus were out putting the fish wheel away, I opened the barrel to get all the fish out. Oh MAN... never having even heard of stink fish let alone smelling them, the name is very appropriate. Good thing they told me to wear gloves. Later that day Remy told me they knew when I was working on the fish because she could smell it where they were working with the wheel across the slough. Now what makes the fish stink is that they ferment and they actually start to degrade and part of them is mush. The reason I was pulling them out of the barrel is so they would not freeze together. The stink fish was going to be cut up and used for dog snacks on the trail and during racing.

There were also two "cribs" of fish at the homestead as well as split fish on a rack. In the cribs the fish also started to ferment and could be pretty stinky as well. What happens is that, in the fall, when the dog salmon are running in the river, they are collected and just piled onto the ground with maybe tin or wood surrounding them in a square. As it is starting to freeze, the smart thing to do is to get all the fish out of the crib and lay them in a single layer to let them freeze separately , then put them back into the crib. If you don't do this then you will have just a frozen clump of fish that takes a lot of chopping with an ax. I did not do this one year and never did it again because slightly fermented, mushy frozen fish are hard to get apart at -40F.

The winter I was at Cletus & Remy's it was -70 for two weeks. I think that was in January. Remember there was only an outhouse. You waited until the absolute last minute to run to the outhouse, do your business and get back into the cabin. No reading the Sears catalog those two weeks. We cleaned up dog poop every day, sometimes twice a day. Those two weeks I could clean up around five dogs and then have to stop to go in for an hour to warm up my hands. They had some pretty hardy dogs because we never lost a dog to hypothermia that winter. I never lost any of mine that time either. That winter we did have to put my leader Sammy down. He had gone blind and deaf. I took a team on a training run while Cletus put him down for me.

I was able to do some training runs on a four-wheeler when I got there, until the snow was too deep for the four-wheeler. We could only go certain trails with the four-wheeler as there were a lot of lakes in the area we could not be on with the four-wheeler. Since they had no snow machine, we had to break open and drag the trail with dogs. What that entailed was, Cletus had taken a big piece of chicken wire and wrapped one end around a log and the other end was cut small and was attached to the sled by tying it to the handlebar and when we took the dogs out on a training run they pulled that drag also.

It worked and I had tough dogs. I was training mostly two-year-olds and one of my own dogs.

There were several people living on homesteads not close as we think of neighbors maybe 5 miles apart or so. I also got to know many people in Manley Hot Springs who I see often even now. Manley is an "end of the road" village. The Elliott highway stops here. (Highway being relative as it is a gravel road from Livengood to Manley) It is full of characters. A lot of people say that people who cannot survive anywhere else move to the end of the road. Alaska has several end of the road communities.

If we needed to make a supply run from the homestead, we would drive the dogs to Manley. Tie them up there and get in the truck and drive the 3.5 hours (on a good day) to town and get supplies. When we would get back from town we would load the supplies in the dog sled and drive the dogs back home. The sled could carry double your weight. I even carried home a 100# propane tank once in the sled.

Most of my trips and training runs with the dogs were uneventful. But there are some stories.

Living out there was the first time in my life I had ever heard deafening silence. Not a single noise and especially when it was really, really cold. I remember one morning I had gone outside and was standing there and heard a chomping noise. We were in the woods so it could have been anything. The dogs were quiet, so I knew it was not them and the noise was not close. I turned toward the slough and there was the cause of the chomping. Two beavers on the ice chopping on a willow. The cold was able to carry that sound up the riverbank.

Back to the little cabin I lived in. The only light was a Coleman lantern. Also, I had not ever up to this point ever heated with a wood stove. I had to master the art of working with a wood stove. Once I got it nice and toasty I went to bed, sometimes I would have it so toasty in there I would have to get up and open the door to cool it off. Once it was back at a good temperature, I would go back to bed and then somewhere in the night the fire would go out and there would be ice inside the cabin in the morning. I will never miss waking up and trying to get dressed in my sleeping bag so I would be somewhat, even if just a little bit warmer, to go down the ladder and start the stove all over again. There were days I could not get it restarted, so I would just throw on my winter clothes. There were a few times when I could not get warm so I would trudge over to the Cletus & Remy's cabin and sit in their living area to warm up.

Starting the "dog pot" every day became one of my chores. Since we had no running water we would go down to the hole in the ice and scoop out water and fill 5-gallon buckets that would have to be brought up the bank (which had snow stairs chopped in it), and fill the dog pot and bring up enough to have drinking and cooking water for my cabin and theirs. It was a chore just to keep the ice water hole open. The hole was originally made with an auger and was covered with a piece of plywood. Each trip to the water hole was a job. You had to chop the ice that had formed at the bottom sides of the hole just so the hole would not completely freeze up. Then scoop out the ice before you could get water. One time around Christmas when Cletus and Remy had gone outside to visit family, I did not do that well enough and the ice hole froze. For a couple of days, I had to melt a lot of snow in the dog pot for dog food. It ended up being A LOT of snow to melt.

A dog pot is half of a 50-gallon drum put on top of another 50-gallon drum with a hole cut in the side. You then have to build a fire in the 50-gallon drum to cook the dog food. The dog food we cooked was salmon and rice and then when that was cooked a little commercial dog food was thrown in . When we started to train the dogs longer miles we would add meat. It is great dog food; the dog utilizes most of it so there is very little poop to clean up.

CHAPTER 6

DOG STORIES

One day I was on a training run. I was only doing 18 miles. I was at the turn around and something happened. I can't remember if a dog had gotten tangled or I had to fix something but I was just going through the turnaround when I had to stop. I set the snow hook and flipped the sled on its side making it harder if the team got away from me. Well..... they did. I hollered for them and of course they did not stop. They are trained to go and when they have less weight on the sled they can really go. I started running. I was 9 miles from home. About 1/4 mile down the trail, I looked up and saw what looked like two figures, in dark jackets, hunched over my team and the team was stopped. Remy had said before I left she might follow with another team. I assumed it was her. I continued to run and as I got closer saw no other dogs other than the team I was running. I was shouting "thank you, thank you. It was not extremely cold but I was not looking forward to walking in the snow 9 miles home. When I got to my team, there was no one around!!. The sled was upright and the snow hook was on the ground, dogs were calm and just standing there. I yelled another " thank you", pulled the snow hook and left.

When I got back, I recounted the story to Remy and Cletus. Cletus told me it was probably "Bushmen".

"Bushman", "Woodsman" (WM) "Nik'inka'eena" (Koyukon), "Naa'in" (Gwich'in). These are all names for a Sasquatch like being who inhabits the Interior. They are known to "take babies", destroy property, and to be unseen. There is a lot of superstition surrounding them and why they live like they do. They are bigger than most humans. There are a lot of stories in the Interior of Alaska about them and there are certain things you do to keep them away from your property. They are not my stories to tell. I asked an elder in Arctic Village who the Naa'in were and he told me that they were the outcasts from a long time ago. I do wish that when I caught up to my team and pulled my snow hook that I had looked for tracks.

We did most of our dog training in the dark. There were two reasons for that. One is that there is limited daylight in the winter. No, it is not dark 6 months of the year like most people believe. The amount of daylight depends on what part of Alaska you are in. If you live in SE Alaska it is more like the winter darkness in Seattle. If you live in the Fairbanks/ Interior area it is light from 10am-2pm and if you are in Utqiagvik (Barrow) it does go dark for one whole month in December.

One has to realize that in Alaska most of the state is covered in snow in the winter so dark is relative. It is not dark, dark like in the Lower 48. Especially in a full moon. The moon reflects off the snow and during a full moon you can walk around without wearing a headlamp or using a flashlight.

The other reason we trained in the dark was because Cletus always slept until about noon so we never got going with the morning chores until then so we sometimes would not start out with teams until dusk. At times we would not get back until 4am. I know this bugged the heck out of Joee Redington Jr. He lived and trained dogs in Manley. He was a sprint musher (short and fast) and he liked to groom his training trail at night so it would "set up" (become hard because of the cold). Sprint mushers like smooth hard trails. Distance mushers never cared so much about that as long as there was a trail of some kind. We would drive the dogs from the homestead to Manley and get on the Tofty road (a mining road) and go. The Tofty road was Joee's main training trail. I remember one night we were coming back from a long run. It must have been 3 am, I was in the back, we were coming down the Tofty road and I looked back because I saw a light and here was Joee on a snow machine behind me dragging his trail. He had seen us go out so he waited until we came back before he went out to drag.

One training run was planned for 100 miles. We were going out 50 and back 50. We left the homestead headed up the Tofty Road toward the trail to Tanana. It started snowing and blowing. We thought we were on the trail and ended up at a miner's cabin. I remember Cletus walking up to the cabin and knocking and a bleary sleepy-eyed miner answering the door and telling us where we were. We got ourselves back on the trail and decided we better stop and water the dogs. No, we had not brought water with us. We cut three spruce poles, made a tripod and hung a bucket with snow in it from the tripod and built a fire underneath. We added some kind of meat or fish, I don't remember and fed it to the dogs. We got to Woodchopper and decided to turn around. Just before getting there Cletus had been looking at the trail, we had just come over and it was snowing so hard it was covering our trail as soon as we made it. The dogs were breaking the trail open ahead. Woodchopper had been a mining town but it was closed during WWII due to the war and had never reopened. There were mines operating all over the district in this area at the time I was there and still are but Woodchopper was never a town again. When I was training dogs there were still a few of the old buildings there. Cletus asked me to go with snowshoes and make some kind of turn around. I walked ahead and did but it was not good enough so he made another one. Back home we went and as we came down the Tofty road, out came Joee trying to groom his trail again that we had gone over.

Another run Cletus, Remy and I were out training. We had about 14 dogs each. I was in the back of the line. We were on our way home and all of a sudden I could not see my team. I knew they were in front of me but a fog had enveloped them.

It had come on so slowly I had not realized it until I could not see my wheel dogs (the dogs closest to the sled). I did feel the air was getting a little colder. When we got home I said something on the offhand about it and was told it was ice fog from the dog's breath. It had dropped into the -40's while we were out. It had been about -10F when we had left home. The condensation that formed from the dogs breathing froze in the air. This happens especially in the Interior of Alaska in the winter when it gets very cold. The condensation caused by car exhaust makes the ice fog so dense that it is hard to see while driving.

One thing I especially learned from dogs was to trust your leader. I had a leader named Lucy. She had originally been a Susan Butcher dog. She was an older dog by the time I was running her. She was one eyed having lost an eye to a branch, I think. I was traveling back home from Manley with the dogs by myself and it started blowing and snowing. We were crossing a frozen lake and Lucy was going a way I did not think was right. I stopped the team, went up and moved her to the part of the lake I thought the trail was on. She stayed where I put her until I pulled the hook to go and then went right back to where she wanted to go. I did this a couple of times then thought "oh what the hell". We crossed the lake and ended up right on the trail on the other side. She knew best!

I had some beautiful training runs. Out at night by myself with a full moon and the Northern lights out. Nothing but the swooshing of the sled runners on the snow and the jingle of the neckline snaps on the dog collars. I remember one particular one where the lights were pure white and coming down from the sky to the ground in sheets. It was so nice not to have to use a headlamp running dogs. You could see so much around you and spot other animals you could not see while having a tunnel of light from a headlamp in front of you.

The most beautiful run I had was on Christmas Day that year. Remy and Cletus had gone Outside for a vacation. I had decided on Christmas Eve I would go to visit Joee and Pam Redington. I ended up spending the night. The next day, I left their house before the sun rose and headed home. It took about 2 1/2- 3 hours to get to the homestead from Manley. As I was crossing the Tanana river and hitting the other shoreline the sky showed me the most gorgeous sunrise. There was a little fog coming off of some open water in the main channel of the river and the sky was yellow and pink but subtle in color like a painting. I was sad when I got home that I could not enjoy watching it anymore but dogs had to be unhooked and the dog pot started. This was the day that the hole had frozen because I had not cared for it properly.

During those months training from the homestead, I had gotten really good at driving a sled.....so I thought. One day coming home with a load of freight from Manley I was coming down a small incline, did not shift my weight right or the sled load shifted, I am not sure but I ran into a tree. Not so bad you might think. Well.... The brush bow, the curved piece of wood in front of the sled banged into the tree breaking and getting the tree caught in it. I can pull this out, I thought, so I tried. The dogs knowing, we were close to home were all pulling in the other direction. I pulled and I pulled and I pulled until I was tired. Finally, the dogs got a little tired of jumping, screaming and going nowhere so they settled down a little bit. I sat down on the sled to think about my predicament. How was I going to get this sled brush bow undone from around the tree? Ahh, I had an ax. I always carried an ax, a 30.30 rifle, sleeping bag, snacks and snowshoes. I pulled out the ax and commenced cutting the tree down. While I was doing this the thought crossed my mind that once the brush bow was free the dogs would take off. I decided I better set the snow hook and also tie off to a nearby tree. There was always a rope attached to the carabiner that hooked the dog's gangline to the sled. Now I had to cut down the tree above the brush bow because I could not swing the ax with any clearance underneath it. So once the tree was down I then had to lift the broken brush bow over the stump to really get it free. I repositioned the snow hook farther out to the right before I made the last two swings toppling the tree. That way I could lift the sled and still have it secured.   All I could envision was the dogs taking off flipping the sled and having all of the freight scattered on the trail from here to home. To my amazement this all worked. Off to home went. Of course, then Cletus was not too happy he had to fix the brush bow.

Sometime between Christmas and the end of February I had a friend come and visit me. Cletus & Remy had taken dogs to Tanana to go visit so Terry and I were at the homestead alone. When his time was up, I was taking him back to Manley, by dog team, to catch his plane back to Fairbanks and then home to Missouri. On the trip we ran into a bunch of moose on an open portage. There must have been 8 or 9 of them. Moose and dogs don't mix. Moose see dogs as wolves, their main predator and they will fight for the trail. Dogs see moose as something to chase. We had not had any indication that there were moose on the portage until we were on top of them. We passed by four as we entered the portage. We were in a time crunch since Terry had to make the plane which only came three times a week. I stopped the team hoping the moose would move off the trail and out of harm's way. The dogs were pulling, screaming, jumping to get at them. Terry was in the sled inside the sled bag. Next to him was my 30.30. The moose were not moving. I decided to try and fire a warning shot. So, I pulled out the rifle, took off the safety and shot into the air. The moose did not move but it scared the dogs who yanked on the sled and flipped it over and started pulling up the trail. Poor Terry, he was still in the sled bag with the sled on its side being pulled face first through the snow and I was dragging, still carrying the rifle. I got the dogs stopped, righted the sled and put the rifle back in the sled bag. Wow, that did not get the result I was hoping for because the moose had not moved. The rule is that if you run into moose who don't move you break a trail way around them. That was not going to work in this instance because the place off to our left had moose and the place off to our right was full of trees and there was no way I could get a team through that thick stand of spruce. I decided to pull the hook and stand on the sled brake and the sled drag with all my weight so that I could slowly move the dogs forward and hopefully the moose would just meander off the trail. IT WORKED!!. We made it to Manley just in time for me to tie up the dog team and walk with Terry to the airstrip to catch the plane. After his plane left I drug my feet getting the dogs ready to make the return trip home. I did not want to run into those moose again by myself. When I got back to that portage the only thing visible were moose tracks. Someone was looking out for me.

CHAPTER 7

QUALIFYING FOR THE IDITAROD

B ack then in order to qualify for Iditarod you had to do 500 miles of qualifying races. I decided upon the Knik 200 and the Copper Basin 300.

KNIK 200

Cletus was to be my handler so we drove down to Wasilla and stayed with some of Cletus' friends. I cannot tell you what my draw number was but we started out. It was to be about 100 miles out to Yentna Station and 100 miles back. I had made it to the Skwenta River. I had about 12 dogs. As I went down the river there were three other teams behind me. We were just trotting along when I saw three snow machines coming down the river. The river is wide and they were spread out. Myself and the other mushers had our headlamps on. As the machines came closer two of them headed over toward the other side of the river and one just kept coming toward us. I saw him coming and he was not stopping or slowing down. His headlight was on so there was no mistaking there were the dogs' eyes reflecting the light and our headlamps shining toward him. He did not swerve until he was on top of my leaders. His left ski hit one of my leaders causing me to lose my footing and get my foot caught underneath my sled , caught between by drag and the sled, throwing me off balance. He did not stop….. probably driving drunk. I was able to get the team stopped and get my leg out. Before I knew it two of the mushers behind me had stopped their teams and ran up to see if we were okay. They stood on my sled and hook so I could run up and check on my dogs. Fortunately, they were unscathed. I did have the vet at the Yentna checkpoint check them out and told the Race Marshall, but the snow machine was long gone.

The layover at Yentna and the trip back were uneventful and I finished 12th, I think. Which is not bad for someone who had not driven a dog team until 3 months before.

COPPER BASIN 300

February brought me to the Copper Basin 300. This race goes from town to town. You are not allowed help during the race but your dog truck and handler can meet you at each checkpoint. Remy and Cletus both came on this trip.

I was racing this race with some well-known names such as Martin Buser, Art Church, Will Forsberg, Jeff King. A few things out of the ordinary happened in this race. When I pulled into the Chistochina checkpoint one of the race officials , Jack, was telling me where to park my team. He was standing right on the trail where it took a turn. After we talked I told my dogs to go ahead, they did but took the corner too sharp, went through the deep snow where Jack was standing, knocking him down and we promptly ran over him. To this day, over 27 years later, whenever I see him, he still reminds me of the incident where I was trying to kill him. When we stopped in Chistochina, it was cold, -40's. An Ahtna woman came to me and said you look cold. I am going to bring you some Indian ice cream at the next stop. I did not know who this woman was until later. She did meet me at the next checkpoint and handed me some Indian ice cream (agutuk).

Agutuk is made differently in each region depending on where you are. In the Interior, which is where we were, it is made from crisco, oil, berries, sugar and sometimes salmon. Some make it with moose fat instead of crisco and oil and in the Northern Interior made with caribou fat. In the village of Nanwalek in South Alaska it is made with fish eggs (another story for another time).

Besides being good it is used as a food in the winter. Your body will generate heat breaking down all the fat and it gives you a lot of energy and warms you up. Well, it did that for me. I am forever grateful to her. I found out later that it was Lena

Charley. She is a very traditional elder and at that time and throughout her life she had dogs she used on the trapline and she also raced

Later on, that race I had to cross a running stream of water. Alaskan huskies, and for that matter any husky does not like water especially when it is running. Well, I had a leader named Hester and the male I cannot remember his name. They were doing great until it came to the water crossing. There was shelf ice on the side of the creek we were going to cross. Shelf ice is a layer of ice that forms when the water is up and then after it freezes, the water drops leaving a ledge of ice. As the leaders were crossing, the shelf broke and they fell into the water. Mind you the water was probably 6 inches deep. Well...they did not like that, they scrambled around getting themselves tangled. Eventually they made it to the other side. It was slightly hilarious as the other side was about 3 feet away. They acted like they had fallen into the ocean. By the time the whole team got to the other side there were several tangles, so I set my hook and went to untangle the leaders first. I got them untangled. I also had to roll the really wet ones in snow. Rolling a wet dog in snow will help dry it off. What I had not realized this whole race or even before the race was that Hester was in heat. So, while I was untangling the other dogs, the male leader thought it was prime time to mount Hester. Well needless to say I had to sit on the sled and wait until that was finished. This caused at least one musher to pass me. After that we nicknamed Hester, Hester the molester, even though she was the one who got molested.

The musher that passed me we all called the Purple Haze. Several of us had already run in with him in this race. There had been several of us lined up behind each other and he was in front. Well, he had to stop and do something to his team and put his sled sideways in the trail so no one could get by. Very unsportsmanlike. Several of us complained to race officials but to no avail.

Well, he passed me at the creek. Right after the creek the trail went up a small mountain, at least that is what it seemed like, his dogs slowed way down. Mine were tougher so we passed him giving him the advantage of the chase. Dogs love to chase. They could act like they are so tired and then you put another team in front of them and it is almost like you injected them with amphetamines. We approached Summit Lake and I was going to rest there. I was ahead of him but as I tried to rest the dogs, which they did not want, Purple Haze passed me again. When I left Summit Lake, I made it my goal to finish before him. It was 30 more miles until the finish line and I think I kicked off the side of the sled for most of that 30 and I beat him. I finished 13th. Had I not stopped at Summit Lake I could have done better, but this was only my second race, so I was pretty proud of my dogs and myself.

I had qualified to run the Iditarod. I have been the only one or one of only a handful that have qualified in the same year as I ran the Iditarod. There is now an Iditarod rule against doing it that way.

I had one more event to do before the Iditarod. Joe Redington Sr. the "Father of the Iditarod" had decided to start a race called the Serum Run. It would actually start in Nenana where in 1925 the dog team relay had started to bring the serum to Nome. This new Serum Run would also be run in relay fashion with each team having a fake box of serum. I was to be part of the relay from Tolovana Roadhouse to Manley. The other mushers with me were Joee Redington Jr and Larry Grout. I am not sure who was the musher that came from old Minto to Tolovana and handed me the serum but I left ahead of Joee and I passed Larry on the trail to Manley. I got to the Manley Hot Springs resort about 10 minutes before anyone knew I was there. I could see people inside but no one to check my time. These were timed relay legs. I ended up finishing second to Joee but not really sure, maybe I did win if someone had been out there!! It really did not matter to me; it was fun and I got a trophy that was probably about 3 feet tall. I no longer have it and never displayed it because it was too big but I do have the plaque from it.

Things began to get busy. Drop bags for the race were required to be shipped out ahead of time. Dog mushers make bags of dog food and other supplies such as socks, batteries, people food, cassette tapes (yes cassette tapes, it was the mid 90s) and other items the musher thought they might need, ahead of time to be sent out to the various checkpoints along the Iditarod race trail. We had to drive into Fairbanks to do this. Remy and Cletus had a friend Marie that lived in North Pole who was going to house us and let us use her place to do these drop bags. Cletus and Remy left the day before or that morning. I was coming in their old truck with Stephanie, who wanted a ride to town. I checked the gas gauge and it was good. When we got to Livengood turnoff, 80 miles from Manley the gas gauge was almost empty. That was weird because we should be able to get to North Pole on one tank of gas. We went into Livengood which is an old mining town. The only thing there in the wintertime is the DOT station. They had gas pumps but would not sell us any. We hoped we could make it to Joy Alaska at 49 mile of the Elliott highway, 20 more miles. This was a very small place with few residents but had a little store, maybe someone would give us gas. We stopped there but they said they had no extra gas. The next place we could go was Hilltop truck Stop about 40 more miles toward Fairbanks. We made it there and got a little gas. Did not fill up, which was a mistake. We were about 30 miles from the North Pole, it was late by then probably 10pm. We were going to stay with Marie's kids at their house. After we left Hilltop the gas gauge just started to plummet. We made it to about a mile from where we were going to stay when we ran out of gas. We had to bundle up and walk to the house and wake them up to get gas so we could get the truck to their house. I can't remember why the truck used so much gas but we never had a problem with it after that.

We got the drop bags finished which took us two whole days. We were making the bags for my team and for Cletus'. We had to cut meat, fat, and chicken up with a band saw and chop stink fish with an ax. We got the drop bags to Fairbanks airport and back to the homestead we went to get everything ready for the race.

CHAPTER 8

IDITAROD

Well, I could not believe I had made it. I attended the rookie musher meeting. There were 59 people signed up. Only 9 women. I was competing in a sport that had been won by two women in the past but was still dominated by men.

My mom, her sister Betty, my Uncle Joe and Aunt Joy came. I also had a friend, from Kentucky, who had just gotten married and she and her husband decided to come to Alaska on their honeymoon to see me race and I had a group of students from Fort Thomas, Kentucky come to cheer me on. The students were studying the Iditarod and had found out I was calling KY my home and had entered from there. They had made books for me that they had sent me. Several of their parents worked for Delta Airlines, so they were able to come up to Anchorage for free. They came to the start and restart to wish me well. Downtown Anchorage is the ceremonial start of the race. It was 1995 and the Alaska Public Health Nurses were using this race to promote their Shots for Tots program. Little did I know that a picture of me that had been taken at the serum run in Manley had been blown up to life size and was being taken around to promote the program, because I was a nurse. I asked a friend who was a nurse to help handle my dogs at the start of the race. She knew I needed other handlers so she recruited all nurses for handlers and they all had Shots for Tots bibs on. I had one other friend Conrad who was an Iditarod veteran helping me and my friend Terry, from the moose incident, was going to ride my second sled. The second sled was used to help slow down the dogs during the ceremonial start. At that time the ceremonial start ran from downtown Anchorage to Eagle River. There are people all along the trail and some who bring dogs so you need that extra help in case you have to stop or people get in the way. It was fun because there were people all along the trail with the newspaper pictures of all the mushers so they would shout out your name. People would hand out hot dogs, soda, cookies and other food to you as you ran by. Many spectators would also use it like a tailgating party and be out there grilling and having a good time. I wish I had been able to take pictures of it all.

The Iditarider program, that year, was either in its first or second year. People could bid on being a passenger in the sled for a few miles. I had a woman from New Hampshire. Things were going well until we made the turn to go down Cordova St. I flipped the sled with her in it. We did not have our full team of 16 dogs for this ceremonial start, which was good, I think I had 10 so they were easy to stop. I got the sled righted and off we went with no other issues on our ride to Eagle River.

The dogs went in the truck and we headed to our host family's house for dinner and sleep. The next day we drove the dogs to Wasilla. There was no way to run from Eagle River to Wasilla because of the water, so we had to truck them. The restart was in Wasilla. It has not been there for a long time due to development and increasing need for housing. At present the Iditarod restarts further north in Willow.

The next day as we were getting ready to do the restart, someone came over to me and said I just saw you at the Immunization trailer. I told them I had not been over there and they said I just saw you and they were laughing. They told me I had to go over there. I could not believe what I was seeing as I was walking up to that trailer…. I was there, a life size cardboard cutout of me in my red snowsuit in front of the public health nursing trailer. Another foreshadowing moment here, this was not the only time during Iditarod I was going to see myself. We were able to leave the Wasilla restart without a full sled as we raced to Knik. At Knik we traded off to the sled we were going to race with. I had a smaller sled that had also been shipped to McGrath. The one I left Knik with was loaded with all the mandatory gear that was going to be checked at each checkpoint; ax, snowshoes, sleeping bag, booties for the dogs, people food and a 24-hour supply of dog food. Anything else was at our discretion.

After all the hoopla with the ceremonial start and the restart I was finally on the trail. It was a great sense of relief to be out there with just the dogs. I remember I had a camera in the bottom of my sled bag and I took one picture on the first stop but never found that camera again the whole rest of the race and had no pictures from the trail. Now, what would Iditarod be without stories so here we go.

The first checkpoint after Knik was Yentna station. If you remember, I had been there during the Knik 200. When you get to a checkpoint you have to stop and let the checkers go through your sled bag to make sure you have all of your mandatory items. I had done that and not planned to stay there but to head onto Skwentna before I stopped for a longer rest. Hester, who had been one of my lead dogs in the Knik 200, was one of my lead dogs for this race. She remembered stopping at Yentna Station during her last time through there so she took a right off the race trail to head to the Roadhouse like she had done before, dragging the rest of the team with her. I was able to stop her halfway up the hill and climbing on the side of the trail through the deep snow. I grabbed her to turn the team around and she was adamant about turning back to the Roadhouse. She did that several times. By then, I was cussing like a sailor. There was a dog musher coming behind me who was very religious and yelled at me for cussing. It was the last thing I needed to be admonished for my language. I finally got Hester back on the trail and off to Skwenta we went. I stayed in Skwentna. Joe and Norma Delia managed the roadhouse and Skwentna. I got there in time so that I could sleep in the roadhouse before it got too crowded.

Sleep, one thing that is precious and you have very little of when running the Iditarod. If you planned to stop for four hours, most of that time was eaten up with dog chores. The first chore was to start heating water for your dog food, laying straw for the dogs to sleep on, checking their feet for splits or redness, then feeding them, then reheating more water to water them before you left the checkpoint. So, in a four hour rest you might get 1-2 hours of sleep. Sleep for me at that time was non-existent. There was a musher there, Dave, who had beat me into the roadhouse and was already asleep and snoring like a Stihl logging chainsaw. So… There went a 24-hour period for me with no sleep. On to Finger Lake. I got there during the day. The sun was up so it was warm outside. When the sun beats on the snow it can warm up fast for the dogs, so I decided we would stop there. I bedded the dogs, did my chores and got a little rest. It is much easier on the dogs to travel at night when it is colder. They really liked -10F to -20F degrees to run in, so we did a lot of running at night. The bad thing about that is you miss a lot of the wonderful scenery. I left Finger Lake at night headed down the trail. I am not sure how far I was, probably at least 10 miles from the checkpoint when a dog I was racing named Squeak went down. I stopped the dogs, ran up to him and he had started to bloat. This can be very dangerous for dogs because most of the time their intestines have started to twist. It is hard to know why this happened. Squeak was a big dog. I had to turn the sled around, rearrange what was in the sled bag in order to fit him in it and run back to the Finger Lake checkpoint. That meant I had to pass teams head on which is not something my dogs were used to because when we trained at the homestead we were the only ones out there. We had practiced a few head on passes but mostly we had practiced passing from behind. We got back to the checkpoint and I hollered for the vet. (There are vets stationed at all the checkpoints). They got the dog and carried him into the vet tent while I parked my team. He was very bloated. They went ahead and stuck a big trochanter needle in his abdomen to let the air out. I stayed there with him and the vets until they were able to get a plane into the checkpoint to get him to Anchorage, about 6 hours later. The Iditarod has a volunteer air force. These volunteers are private pilots who volunteer their time and planes to move dogs, supplies and people along the trail. This put me behind about 8 hours. When I knew the plane was there I went back to the team and got them headed down the trail again. (Squeak survived and went on to run other Iditarods in Cletus' team).

The Happy Valley, about 10 miles from Finger Lake, is well known to mushers. We call it the Happy Valley steps. The trail goes down, levels, goes down, levels, goes down, you get the idea. Me having started number 53, I was still in the last half of the group and the trail was well worn through those "stairs". It was sled wide and if you did not hit it right in the sled tracks on your way down it was easy to flip. That did not happen but a few other weird things did. I was making my way down the stairs, it was dark. I heard people talking. I stopped thinking that's weird, I had not passed anyone and there was no one close. When I stopped the talking stopped. Hmm, must have been hearing things. I headed down the next set of "stairs" and heard women laughing. I stopped again..... nothing. Then it dawned on me, I was hallucinating. I had not had much sleep since leaving Knik and was probably a little dehydrated. This story is not unusual. There have been many mushers with stories about seeing animals and people not there. The lack of sleep, food and dehydration all have a play in that.

I went through the Dalzell Gorge with no problems. That area is very problematic depending on the snow level during the year. I did have to ride on some sidehills which was hard for me to do keeping more weight on the uphill side of the runners.

I remember heading through the Alaska Range on my way to Rainy Pass. There was no other team around, We had just come up an incline, made a small left turn and were on a straight part of the trail when out of the snow popped the most beautiful cross fox I have ever seen. He had a large silvery white and black ruff around his face. He sat there not moving a muscle as we went by just following us with his eyes. The dogs did not pay him any attention. After we passed him, I looked back and he curled right back up onto the snow with the sun glinting off his fur. As we were going through the Range, I felt like my team and I were just little ants among these huge mountains. It was a beautiful day, hardly any clouds and beautiful sun. I wish I could have stopped and stayed all day just drinking in the scenery. I got to Rainy Pass and proceeded to get sick. Like the flu sick. I know right before the race I had been tense trying to get everything together and I was nervous about the race start and then there was the Squeak incident. I think by the time I got to Rainy Pass the tension was gone and my body just had enough of that, little sleep and dehydration and decided I needed to rest. I lost about 24 hours there because I just did not feel good and I had to sleep. I also started taking some of the dog amoxicillin I had in my bag. I felt better after resting for 24 hours. So now I was 36 hours behind where I wanted to be but really for me, it did not matter. I was not really "racing". I wanted to get to Nome but most of all I wanted to have the experience. Less people have completed the Iditarod than have climbed Mt. Everest and I was going to be one of them and to be one of only 9 females in the race, all the more important.

Once I finally left Rainy Pass, things went well . I made it to Rohn and after that ended up at night in a place called the Buffalo tunnels. I decided to stop here and rest. A lot of times we would not stop and stay in checkpoints but out on the trail. I was laying on my sled sleeping and I was woken up by things crashing through the brush. I never did see anything, it was dark, but there is a reason the place is named Buffalo tunnels. They seemed to be moving all around me.

Not long after that, in the pitch dark, no moon I was crossing a creek/stream with shelf ice. Remember what I said about dogs and shelf ice. Well, the leaders tangled with the swing dogs (the dogs behind the leaders). I stopped the sled, set the hook and went up to the leaders, they had crossed the water but in my sleep deprived state, when I was untangling I unclipped the tug line and the neckline of one of the leaders and off she ran. Her name was Goldie, she was missing an eye. The other leader I had up there running with her was Lucy and she was missing the opposite eye. Now what was I going to do? I had to find Goldie. It was my worst nightmare, having a dog disappear, because you really could not continue in the race missing a dog. I got the other dogs untangled and the next thing I know here was Goldie standing back at my side. Whew, I just breathed a big sigh of relief. I really needed her as a lead dog, because I had dropped Hester a few checkpoints back when it became very obvious she was pregnant from her shenanigans during the Copper Basin race.

On my way to Nikolai, we traveled along the Kuskokwim River. I ran into a moose on the river, fortunately the snow was not deep and he moved off. As we advanced further down the river, the banks on either side of the river became taller. At one point my dogs kept looking up on the right side to the bank, the hair on the back of their necks came up. It stayed that way for a long time with them looking continually at the bank with hackles up. The only thing I could think of was that we had a wolf or wolves following us because not long after that we came upon a wolf-killed moose on the side of the trail.

Things went well after that until leaving the old mining town of Ophir. As I was going up the hill just outside the town, the sled started to track to the left and over the side of the hill I went. The sled flipped, and I was flipped into the deep snow, and the dogs were floundering in the snow. It was a mess. When I stood up I was in thigh deep snow. There was no way I was going to be able to right the full sled in thigh deep snow. Fortunately, I was able to dig out my snowshoes. Strapping them on, I started getting things out of the sled and carrying them up the side of the hill to the trail. Once I got the sled emptied, I moved the leaders as far up the side of the hill to the trail as I could, went back to the sled, righted it and called to the dogs to go and they pulled us out of the deep snow and back onto the trail. I loaded everything back in the sled, unbuckled the snowshoes and stored them on the sled. We started going again and all of a sudden the sled slid and back down the side of the hill we went. I noticed as we were sliding, I saw other sled tracks that had done the same thing. Come to find out it was the musher in front of me. I again had to strap the snowshoes on and do the same thing. This time when I was back on the trail, Robbie Roberts (the Loafer from Ophir) was coming down on a snow machine and we stopped to talk. I had told him about my experience and he told me a way to use the snow hook to not slip off the hill again. I am grateful for his advice. As I was rounding the corner further up on the trail the sled wanted to do the same thing again and I used the snow hook in the fashion Loafer told me to and saved myself from going over the edge again. I was so glad to pull into the old, abandoned town of Iditarod, the next checkpoint. I pulled in just before it got dark. I was able to see the old remaining mining buildings in the ghost town. It is my goal to one day fly in there again and just explore.

Things from Iditarod to Shageluk went well. It was a beautiful trip. A lot of ups and downs but nevertheless awesome scenery of the Innoko river area.

Up to this point I had been traveling by myself. There are times in this race where mushers travel together. After I left Shageluk I began traveling with Max Hall from England. I remember his leader was named Norway because I always heard him calling out to his leader. At one point Max's headlamp quit working. It was still a dark moon. Fortunately, I had an extra for him to use. We traveled together for quite a while. We parted ways in Kaltag where we stopped for the night. The next morning, I started getting my team ready to leave Kaltag before dawn but did not leave until dawn. It was blistering cold that night and early morning. I was trying to get booties on all of my dogs and had to go back inside the Tribal hall, which was the checkpoint, three times in order to warm my hands up to continue putting booties on. I had one of those zipper thermometers on my parka and the lowest it went was 50 below zero, and the red part of the thermometer had gone past that number. It was COLD!! As I was making my way from Kaltag to Unalakeet the lack of sleep really started to affect me. I would fall asleep on the sled and the next thing I knew the sled had flipped on its side waking me up. I remember this happened three different times.

Prior to the race, living in the Bush and surviving I had lost weight. I lost more on the race because eating was not the most appealing thing to do when I stopped to rest. The most appealing thing to do when I rested the dogs was to get some sleep myself. I had packed a lot of things to eat, frozen strawberries, nuts, dried moose, dried salmon, moose intestine fat, and Twinkies. I really learned how many preservatives were in Twinkies when they did not freeze at 50 below!! When you are in the cold like that for a long time your body craves fat. Stories of mushers eating full sticks of butter is a real thing. We had taken moose gut fat for that purpose. The whole race I could not bring myself to eat any of it and when I arrived at the Bering Sea village of Elim, I gave all my moose gut fat to the Elders.

I arrived in the village of Unalakleet and was stopping there to rest. Coming into that area I had one of my beaver mitts ripped off the string by a branch. I could not retrieve it as I would have had to stop the team and walk backwards to get it. Something a dog musher never does!! The musher behind me did not pick it up because he thought it was an animal. Fortunately, I was able to borrow some mitts for the rest of the race, otherwise my hands would have gotten so cold that I would have really suffered frostbite. I was sad too because that was the first and only pair of beaver mitts I had sewn all by myself. When I got to the checkpoint in the village

I went into the building they had for the mushers to rest. There were fax machines in all the village checkpoints so family and friends could send messages and well wishes to the mushers. Someone approached me and said, "you have a bunch of faxes". They handed me a stack of faxed pictures stapled together. I began to look through the pictures and it was pictures of me at the Nome Alaska Airlines counter, on Front street in Nome, coming out of the bathroom, pictures of me with mushers who had already finished the race. I think I stood there dumbfounded and extremely sleep deprived. It took me a while to realize it really wasn't me, it was that cardboard cutout of me that somehow had made it to Nome from Wasilla. Someone had flown it up there! It ended up making an appearance at the musher banquet, and on the Alaska Airlines jet back to Anchorage and eventually to Joee Redington's training trail back in Manley where it finally deteriorated many years later. The rest of the way to Nome was uneventful.

It was a little surreal as I had mentioned earlier to stop at the Safety checkpoint, where for several years before I had been the checker. My friend Betsy from Nome had snow machined out there to meet me when I got there. As I arrived at the Nome City limits I was still on the Bering Sea ice. People drive about 5 miles outside the city to watch the mushers on the ice. I remember seeing Cletus & Remy waving to me as Cletus had finished two days or so earlier. It was then I realized the race was over. I stopped the team, thanking each one of the dogs for bringing me this far. We climbed up from the trail on the sea ice to Front street and headed for the Arch, the burled arch signaling the finish line. I was sad thinking that my time out in the bush for 13 days traveling with dogs was over and that in a month I would be back in Kentucky, back at work. It was an elated feeling actually finishing the race. Out of the nine women that started the race, six of us finished. It was not my last race but it was my only Iditarod. as the song goes, I did, I did, I did the Iditarod trail!

CHAPTER 9

KENTUCKY

I had decided to go back to Kentucky and live. Shipping 19 dogs via Alaska Airlines. Half of them did not come the day I did but were delivered to me the next day. It was a difficult transition for me back to civilization. I was renting an old farmhouse that sat right under Interstate 64. Going from deafening silence to the noise of traffic was something I really had to get used to. It was hot. The dogs were having a hard time so someone got for me, a large metal pole structure with black shade cloth over the top. This helped cool the dogs off. I got a four-wheeler and I set out training dogs again the following winter. Where I lived in KY was farm country so there were big farm fields I could train dogs in. I had to get permission from all of the neighbors but they were happy to let me use the land to train. I signed up for a few races including the Mackinaw Mush on Mackinac Island Michigan and the Elton 80 in Wisconsin. Both I enjoyed tremendously and returned several times to the Elton 80. I had a great host family there. When I moved back to Ky on Buzzard Roost road, I met a neighbor Judy Young who became a best friend and also became my dog handler. She would ride on the 4-wheeler with me during training and she went with me both times to the Elton 80 to help. In 1996, I decided to run the 1997 International Rocky Mountain Stage Stop Sled Dog race.   It is held in Wyoming every year. It is now known as Pedigree Stage Stop Race. Back in 1997 it was 10 days with one rest day. It was run from town to town in Western Wyoming. You had a host family in every town every night and the town always put on a meal. We did have two overnight stays during the race, meaning we had to camp out with the dogs. At that time this race was also classified as an Iditarod qualifier. The first year I ran it, the old guard, as I call them, were also running it. People like Susan Butcher, Libby Riddles, Rick Swenson, Jacques Philip, Bob Holder.   I will never forget every night at the musher meeting in every town race director Frank Teasley would always say " the trail tomorrow is relatively flat". At the end of the race that year, we bought Frank a level, so he could know what flat really was!!! I also remember that Frank, at each town's dinner, would call Jacques Philip to the front of the room just so Jacques could say "howdy partner" in his French accent. For us flatlanders, those from the Lower 48 and from the Fairbanks Alaska area, we never really trusted what Frank said since we would climb sometimes 3,000 feet in elevation every day. The trail started anywhere between 6,000-8,000 above sea level every day. I remember one stage was so steep,

I felt if I got off the sled it would slide backwards. During those early years there was also a veterinarian who traveled each stage by snow machine and carried oxygen for the dogs. I would joke that I needed the oxygen, not the dogs.

I got to know the trail sweep (the person who followed the last team) very well as I was, most of the time, the last team. I was competing with top mushers who had way more miles on their dogs and were training in snow, but I was very proud of my team to finish the race having trained only on 4-wheeler and no more than 30 mile runs and with no snow.

The scenery running through the Teton and Bridger Mountains and Shoshone National Forest was just breathtaking and the trails were awesome. During one of the days while I was racing I looked over to the left and about 1000 feet into a clearing were roughly 300 head of elk. Beside the Iditarod, I think this race had the most awesome scenery.

My friend Judy and my friend Linda from Alaska came to be my handlers. At that time, you needed two handlers. Once the team left from the start line, the dog truck had to be driven to the next town. In Wyoming in winter, a lot of the passes are closed so sometimes for the fastest mushers their dog truck was not at the finish line when they arrived. The trucks sometimes had to drive 6 hours to get to the next town due to road conditions and closures. I was exhausted when I finished that race. I told Judy I would never do it again. Famous last words...... 1999 we made the trip again. I was not as fortunate in that race. I came with fewer dogs and had several injuries, so I scratched at Pinedale that year but we followed the whole race after I scratched helping out other teams and the race crew.

HANDLERS

I did not have a dog handler when I was training dogs. I did all the chores by myself, feeding, cleaning poop, training. But when I did the Stage stop race in Wyoming I always had two. Handlers can be indispensable when doing a race like this. It takes a special person to be a handler. You have to love dogs, like smelling like dogs, not mind the smell of dog poop or the smell of rotten fish and cooked meat. My friend Judy was one of these people. If it were not for her and my friend Linda Oxley, I don't think I would have made it in that race. Judy drove out west with me both times I did the Stage Stop. We went out a week or so early the first time to try and get the dogs acclimated to the altitude. I have to say they adjusted better than me. I knew we were going to have to do some training runs while there and I wanted Judy on a second sled behind me since I did not know the trails or the terrain. The second sled would be tied to mine. I have to say, it is much harder being the second sled driver because the second sled can really whip around the corners, especially when you are going downhill around a corner. In order to get Judy used to riding a second sled we practiced before we left Kentucky. I had a small sprint sled that I tied to the back of my 4-wheeler and we went into a farm field and I drove around, and went fast while turning to simulate what it would feel like on a second sled. I did knock her off once or twice and I remember that one of those times she fell off but held on to the sled. When I realized she was off I stopped and she got up her glasses askew and dirt on the side of her face but she was proud she had not let go. Her husband Bill told me that he wasn't going to let her play with me anymore!. Judy did great riding the second sled in Wyoming. She only flipped one time, coming down a hill.

Besides being a good dog handler, she is a great friend. We were traveling to Wyoming that first year and we went to Rawlins or should I say about 1 mile from the Rawlins exit and traffic came to a halt. The wind was terrible and it was snowing. There was a tractor trailer beside us and the trailer was just rocking in the wind. All I could imagine was that trailer flipping over. If you readers have never been out west, there is no wind like there is out west. There is nothing to stop it on the prairie. We were stopped for a long time. I could see the exit sign for a rest area that was one mile up the road. The longer we sat there the more I had to pee. I began to see I was not the only one who was having that issue. I started seeing a few women trying to brave the wind to make it to the rest area. I was NOT about to do that so here we were trying to figure out how to remedy that situation. Judy finally handed me a gallon Ziploc bag. I wiggled off my coat, put it under me so I would not get the seat wet and proceeded to empty my bladder into the bag. When we went to the rest area, she took the bag and disposed of it. Now that is a true friend.

MONTANA

I stayed in Kentucky for 5 years and then packed up and moved to Montana. I went to Anaconda and rented a house in downtown Anaconda. It was across the street from the foundry and when it rained the puddles in the yard had a very pretty sheen of green. Anaconda, for those of you who don't know, was a copper smelter town and the smelter stack is still there along with the large slag pile I don't think will ever go away. I worked at the Anaconda Community Hospital. That was a type of hospital I should have worked in when I was just out of school. It was a rural hospital. In a 12 hour shift you could be working in the ER for a couple of hours, then in ICU, then on the regular floor and then OB. I did learn a lot being on OB call and it was an experience that helped me greatly later in my career. I made some lasting friendships there even though most of the time outsiders were not accepted. The community was originally more of an immigrant community that had come to work in the smelter business and according to some of the older people the town was divided depending on your nationality and one nationality did not like the other. Several of my friends told me later that the reason a lot of Anaconda people did not like outsiders, they thought they would take their job. This was a thought leftover from the smelter days. The smelter closed in 1980 and I was there in 2000. 20 years and there was still that mentality among some.

I only stayed in the house across from the Foundry for a month then found a rental at Georgetown Lake. A beautiful place and both places that I rented there were awesome. You can't touch a house there now since the Californians have discovered Montana. Up around Georgetown Lake there are several abandoned mines. Southern Cross, Red Lion and past Red Lion was the old Philipsburg silver mine. The second house I lived in there was on Red Lion road, it had a great access for dog mushing and the trail took me by Red Lion mine and I would turn around at the old Philipsburg mine. At night you could hear coyotes and occasionally a wolf. I could watch young bull moose in the open field by the house play sparring. I had the sled dogs there. Sometimes the dogs would bark so much I would go to look out the window and there might be 1-4 black bears just moving around the yard, looking in the guest house door, undeterred by the dogs. Or another time there might be a moose eating on the bale of straw in the back of the truck. Elk roamed the area as well. It was one of the best places I have ever lived. I did travel a lot to other states to race my dogs when I lived at Georgetown Lake and even put on a race for a couple of years called the Pintler Turkey Run.

CHAPTER 10

GOING BACK

In 2005 the wanderlust hit me again, life was changing for me (I was getting ready to go through my second divorce) so I decided to look to Alaska again. I loved where I was living in Montana and the job was okay. I was only working three 12 hour shifts a week but something was pulling me back. It seems like Alaska was always my escape place. I searched online and I saw a job for an itinerant Public Health Nurse based in Fairbanks. It would be the same type of job that I had in Nome, just in Athabascan Indian villages.

So, here I went again. This time packing up everything and a team of dogs. Judy flew out to drive with me and a friend from Montana drove the U-Haul.

Fortunately, the trip was uneventful but the drive up the Alaska Highway was superb. The scenery and the animals, everyone needs to do the trip. Put it on your bucket list.

I ended up renting a VERY small cabin from some friends in Salcha and keeping my sled dogs at their house about a mile away. I am appreciative of them but that got old really quick. I was able to find a house to buy in Two Rivers. My old stomping grounds from the early years. It is always nice, as a dog musher, to have trails outside your door so you do not have to truck your dogs somewhere before you can run them. I was working full time and training dogs.

Having the varying experience that I did at the Anaconda Hospital gave me a more solid background in sometimes being the only medical provider in the villages. The Community Health Aide program was still present but finding and keeping staff was a lot harder now than it had been many years before in Norton Sound. The years of health aides staying in that job for almost their entire adult life were gone. There are very few CHAs in regions of Alaska that have been there for 30+ years.

I was able to do a lot more health teaching in the schools than I had at Norton Sound, which is a part of the job I loved.

It was such a Godsend to be able to go back to Alaska to one of the best jobs I have ever had.

Always in the woods
with a gun.
Blueberry picking
with Linda Johnson
on the Yukon River

Sledging the dogs to
Tanana village
carnival to race

On the trail with
Linda Johnson
traveling to work in
Tanana

CHAPTER 11

PUBLIC HEALTH NURSING IN THE INTERIOR

I went to work for Fairbanks Regional Public Health Center. I was classified as a Public Health Nurse III. Those with my classification were the itinerants, the ones that traveled. We did not see any patients in Fairbanks, only in the villages where we were assigned. My new job had me covering the villages of Arctic Village, Venetie, Fort Yukon, Beaver, Stevens Village, Chalkyitsik, Rampart and Tanana. They are Gwich'in and Koyukon Athabascan villages.

When we were fully staffed there were four Itinerant nurses. Each one of us was responsible for a different region. We were only fully staffed for about four or five years. After that it was hit and miss but I was able then to cover more villages and see the different cultures in the villages. I was assigned what is called the Fort Yukon subregion. Fort Yukon was the hub village and I had a clerk that worked for Public Health Nursing that lived and worked there. I had an office in the clinic in Fort Yukon that I shared with her.

Fort Yukon is a village of 500-600 depending on who you are talking to. It is Gwich'in Athabascan. At one time it had a population of 1,000+. That was when the Air Force Base was there. Part of the base is still there and there are a few people that operate out of the base but a lot of it is gone. Fort Yukon and Galena had Air Force bases that were operational during the Cold War. Alaska also had many DEW lines/ White Alice sites along its Western coast that were also operational during the Cold War. Most of these have been abandoned for many years and some have been torn down.

The clinic in Fort Yukon is staffed with mid-levels and occasionally has an MD employed. There is a quasi-ER there. Most severe traumas, cardiac, broken hips etc. are medevaced out to Fairbanks, Anchorage, Seattle or Salt Lake depending on the need. This is true for all Alaskan villages. Things can get kind of dicey when the weather goes down and the medevac planes cannot make it in. There have been instances when the medevaced could not make it in due to weather and it was imperative that the person get out of the village for medical care. In those instances, the Army stepped in and sent their MAST helicopter out to pick up a patient and transport them to Fairbanks or take them to a bigger village where the weather was not so bad and the medevaced would pick them up from there.

Fort Yukon sits on the Yukon River and relies on subsistence king salmon fishing to supplement their diet. King salmon, moose, geese, berries, were the subsistent foods that were mainly eaten. Now they are supplements to the diet. King Salmon fishing right now has been closed for two years, due to declining numbers. There is a grocery store which has very limited fresh fruit and vegetables. Fresh fruits and vegetables are hard to get into the Bush and very expensive and taste like water or cardboard.

The Porcupine River flows into the Yukon here in this area, also there is the Black River and up the Black River is the village of Chalkyitsik. Chalkyitsik is also Gwich'in Athabascan and probably has 60 people in the village. It was the home of Traditional Chief David Salmon. I had the pleasure of working and learning from him while he was alive.

Northwest of Fort Yukon on the Chandalar river is the village of Venetie. The people of Venetie, about 180 of them, are also Gwich'in Athabascan. Most of the older people in the Gwich'in Athabascan villages do not speak English as their first language. Further North of Venetie is the village of the Neet'sai Gwich'in in Arctic Village. Population here is about 150. I think it is the prettiest of the villages in the Fort Yukon subregion as it sits in the Eastern Range of the Brooks Mountains and in the Alaska National Wildlife Refuge. Venetie and Arctic Village did not participate in the Land

Claims Settlement so the land is still theirs, all of it.. and they are not subject to Alaska Fish and Game or Federal Fish and Wildlife Management when it comes to caribou hunting or fishing. Also, Venetie and Arctic Village held Federal Reservation status until 2015 where there was a Supreme Court decision to not recognize them anymore. I have tried to find out why but no one I have talked to can really tell me and trying to read the Supreme Court decision was way above my education level!!

The residents of both of those villages still consider themselves as a Reservation. Each one of these villages has a store but is very, very limited in what is offered there. You can buy pop, candy, frozen food, and some canned food. They always have spam and pilot bread.

Going down river from Fort Yukon is the village of Beaver. The people are a mix here of Gwich'in, Inupiaq Eskimo, Koyukon Athabascan and Japanese. The founding of the village is an interesting story that I won't relate here but you can Google it.

Further down river is the village of Stevens Village. Now the population is probably 40. It is Koyukon Athabascan.

Continuing on down river past the Yukon River bridge is the village of Rampart. When I first went there, they had a population of 10. There were several elders there and it was fun to visit them and hear stories of the River in the old days. Koyukon Athabascan here as well. This village has gotten larger as families moved in and the school reopened. Rampart was the last village to get electricity and that was in the 1980s.

The next village down river is Tanana. It is Koyukon Athabascan. It has a population of maybe 250. There used to be a Fort here and there was a hospital here at one time. During the early days this was a hub for the river villages because it had a hospital. A lot of the people up and down the Yukon were born at the hospital that was here. It was still standing when I first went to Tanana and it was a landmark on the River if you were traveling by boat. It has since been torn down. The clinic here is usually staffed by a local mid-level and the health aide. That was as far downriver as my region went for nursing.

There is one more village. It is south of Fort Yukon as you are flying back to Fairbanks. It is the village of Birch Creek. Population maybe 15.

With the exception of Tanana and Fort Yukon all the other villages have Community Health Aides as their medical provider. Arctic Village does get a mid-level every two weeks.

This time I was traveling, I was more outspoken and not shy so I did participate in a lot of what was going on in the villages. This will be more described later but the coolest thing was radio bingo in Arctic Village. People in Arctic Village prior to a cell phone tower being put in did not have landlines or cell phones and only used handheld radios. Actually, I think everyone still has their radio. So, one day they would decide to have a bingo game, usually for a fundraiser for a family who had someone die or was in the hospital or for a spring carnival. They would announce it on the handheld radio and if you wanted to play you would let them know and they would bring around the cards by snow machine in winter or 4-wheeler in the summer. The game would start at a certain time. The caller would announce the numbers over the handheld and if you got Bingo, the runner would come to your house - by snow machine or 4-wheeler and check your card.

The only way for me to get to work from Fairbanks was to fly. As I have said most of my work was in the villages, when I was in my office in Fairbanks, it was a little boring once I finished up all the paperwork from my village trips.

When I started work in Fairbanks my boss just happened to be a boss I had in Nome when I was going to work there per diem. The only orientation I had was to know how the State worked things in Public Health. You know endless paperwork and policies and procedures. I had orientation for a week and then I was sent off to the villages to start working. As with my job in Nome we carried the clinic with us. Unlike Nome though, we had a lot of villages with no health aide and the clinic had not been kept up so I traveled with 8-10 bags each trip. There were two Bush airlines that flew to the villages that I covered and I got to know the pilots very well. I was able most of the time to sit up in the co-pilot seat. At the beginning I would stay in the schools. They always had room and there was always running water. That was not necessarily the case as I have said before in the village clinics. Even in 2005 and after there were still clinics that had no running water. The schools also had kitchens where I could cook my food. I had worn myself out on spam. That and pilot bread had been all I ever traveled with when I was working out of Nome and still to this day I will not eat Spam.

I tried to become more engaged in the Village life this time around, I saw a difference I had not noticed in the Eskimo communities of the North. There was a definite dividing line in the River villages for acceptance. What I mean is that it did not take long for people to trust or talk to me in the Fort Yukon and northern villages but when I went to Tanana it seemed like it took several years of trips before I was accepted. It eventually became a second home to me but in the years since then I think I have discovered maybe the reason for all of that. The influx of non-natives , trappers, traders, miners came via the Bering Sea up the Yukon River, bringing disease and other things that had a detrimental effect on the population. I have always wondered if the distrust had come from that history, maybe not something that people really notice that they are doing but a bred in suspicion of newcomers.

In the years since I started the job the elders have gradually died. The last elder in Tanana passed away in 2022. It is sad to think of all the knowledge that has died with them and with their parents and grandparents. As with all cultures if we don't share the knowledge we have with others that knowledge will die with us.

CHAPTER 12

VILLAGE STORIES

W hen I started working again in Fairbanks, in July 2005, I started keeping a journal, at least for a little while. Here are some of the stories. I hope you find them interesting.

The first fall I started working in Fairbanks, I was making a trip to Arctic Village. My clerk, Laurie, who was based in Fort Yukon came with me. A few days before we were to leave on this trip Laurie called to let me know that the village had run out of fuel. This was an ongoing problem for a couple of years. Fuel comes to most of the villages that are not on the road system or on the Yukon River via a DC-6 (plane). The village tries to anticipate how much they are going to need but when it runs out sometimes the village does not have the money right away to get fuel, or if they owe the fuel company money they won't deliver. So, since the village had run out of fuel, that meant there was no power in the village and no phone. Gas is needed to run the generator at the power plant and for the phone. The school district orders their own fuel and they were not having this problem. We were scheduled to stay in the school anyway and so I decided Laurie and I would still go. The main purpose for this trip was Tuberculosis (TB) screening, hearing and vision screening for the school. I was also going to do mass flu shots and catch up on child immunizations. The village had no trained health aide at the time. Since there were no phones working the town communicated with handheld radios. No one was really expecting us. The trip on the plane was breathtaking especially when we left Venetie headed for Arctic Village. We went from Boreal forest in Venetie to tundra then back to a treed area again. (The trees in Arctic Village are black spruce). The Arctic is surrounded by the mountains of the Brooks Range.

As soon as we landed at the airstrip snow machines roared to the plane to pick up passengers, freight and mail. When we stepped out of the plane our nose hairs froze, indicating to me that it was below zero. One saving grace for this village is most of the people have wood stoves in their home, so they are at least warm even if the village is out of fuel. Many people do have Coleman lanterns so they do well even with no fuel. We attended a school assembly where before and after I gave flu shots. I even gave flu shots on the plane. The people here rely on the caribou for their main source of meat. Most of the villagers are very friendly and are extremely appreciative of the medical services. I was given dried caribou meat by a mom whose child I helped get counseling and I was given a fresh caribou ham by another woman. We did home visits on all of the elders in the village. I did dressing changes in the homes with a headlamp. We were out running around in the village until late at night just visiting. We had supper with an elder who made us a large pot of caribou soup. Villagers stopped by visiting the elder during dinner. Conveniently I had brought my flu vaccine with me so I was giving flu shots there as well. The next night someone brought Laurie some dried caribou meat and a stick of butter. A weird combination I thought. I watched as Laurie took a piece of dry meat and ran it over the butter and ate it. I thought it was the funniest thing…then I tried it. No wonder my cholesterol is over 200!

The next month, I tried to get to Stevens Village but the flight was canceled. Maybe because I was the only paying passenger. The next day the flight was two hours late leaving. By the time I got to the school to do the TB tests the children had already left. I had to call all the parents and have them bring them back. The parents were not long in coming. The word had spread that I was also giving flu shots. I was staying at the school and I had people coming in most of the evening. The next day I did hearing and vision screening at the school and then went over to the clinic to do well child exams and immunizations. Those of you who know by now I will do anything to give shots. I meet men under streetlamps, in unfinished houses, on street corners of the village, construction shacks, all to get them to get their flu shots.

The school is small and so only has two teachers. One is the principal teacher, all for K-12, the other a teacher aide. The principal teacher walked out unannounced the week before I got there. The assistant superintendent from Fort Yukon had flown in to fill in. Part of the reason the teacher had left was because there was no teacher housing and the teacher had to live in the school, not the best situation.

I went from Stevens Village to Rampart. Rampart, at that time in 2005 had about 15 residents. 14 adults, one small child and one pregnant woman. They only got a plane Monday, Wednesday and Friday. The school here closed in the 1980s (but reopened in 2015). It was a very slow trip. I only saw three patients. I did make two home visits. One man I visited had a very interesting house and he was a very interesting individual. His name was Dan. He lived in a log cabin that looked like it was sinking into the permafrost. If you looked at the cabin from the side, the roof had a sway like the back of an old saddle broke horse. When you walked into his home, there were empty commodity cereal boxes stacked floor to ceiling in the corner of the kitchen. There were a lot of empty containers on the kitchen counter. As I walked into the living room I could not help but notice the hose running from a hole in the floor under the door to the outside. The room had a lot of mining memorabilia and it smelled like a mixture of motor oil and mildew. He told me a lot of the history surrounding the village and about what happened on the Yukon River when the 1964 earthquake happened over 800 miles away. He explained to me that the river changed course after the earthquake and part of his cellar collapsed. It fills with water sometimes now and that is the reason for the hose, to pump out water back into the river. His house was the only one with a cellar. He told me that across the river a long time ago there had been an experimental strawberry farm. There were many different types grown there so it could be determined what type did well in the Arctic. Looking across the river now you would never know it had ever been there, the forest has taken the land back. Dan told me where Wyatt Earp's cabin was. At that time, it was still standing. I was amazed to hear that Wyatt had even been there. The story goes that Wyatt stopped in Rampart and stayed a while when he was traveling, via steamboat, to the Bering Sea. He had been to the Klondike but had not struck gold so soon made his way to Nome following gold in the late 1800's. Wyatt eventually made it to Nome starting the Dexter saloon, which during my time in Nome in the early 1990s, was still standing.

I returned back to Fairbanks and the next day was eventful.

I had given two of my sled dogs to a guy from Arctic Village and his teacher girlfriend. They had come into town for the Athabascan Fiddlers Convention and picked the two they wanted to take. The teacher called me about 11:30 am to tell me that they were at the airport and one of the dogs had gotten loose and they could not catch it. I immediately hopped in the car and sped to Fairbanks (30 miles from home). By the time I got there the dog, Brokaw, was nowhere in sight. We looked for a while and then went to Wright Air Service and left a picture of him in case he came back. Just as we were walking out the door Brokaw streaked by on the other side of the road. I ran out and called to him and then he thought it was a game. Up and down the road he ran, in and out of the other air service parking lots, onto the airstrip. Finally, I was able to corner him between two refrigerator vans. I was grateful they took him and the other dog because they were unable to keep up with my team and I would rather have them die running on a trapline team than sitting on a chain in the yard.

That December (2005) I had to make an emergency trip to Chalkyitsik. There was an active TB case. Unfortunately, the patient had symptoms for one month prior to the State epidemiology office getting the chest x-ray and sputum results. I flew out to start her on 4 drug therapy. In the state of Alaska, there has to be a person who watches the patient take their TB medicine for the entire time they are on medication which can be up to a year. That is a hard thing to find even when the State is paying that person $10.00 per day just for the two minutes it takes to watch the patient take their meds. I finally got someone to agree to do it. The village did not have a regular health aide. That would usually be the person who would do it as part of their job. I did have to do a TB investigation and contact list and give TB tests to all those who had been in contact with the patient. This would be repeated in 3 months. Two of the contacts were in another village so I contacted the health aide in that village and they followed up with them.

I was invited the first night to a home for caribou stew and cake to celebrate a couple's 15th anniversary. That night the clinic was cold; they could not regulate the heat so I was very cold sleeping there on the floor. The patients did not stop coming until 9:30 pm. I had arrived earlier in the day at 2:00pm and the sun was already starting to set. It was a brilliant red and orange and even some of the villagers were out taking pictures. I did not get any pictures but I did get pictures of the sunrise the next morning at 10:00am. The sky was yellow, orange and red with wispy clouds that were reflecting the red color. It was pretty mild temperature wise. I don't think it got any lower than 10 above. The second night I slept in an unoccupied teacher's apartment which was nice and warm but even patients found me there at night. The school had their Christmas program, so I went. There was then a big turkey dinner for the community that was donated by the school district. It had originally been for Thanksgiving but did not arrive in time so they saved it for Christmas. I flew back to Fairbanks and it was 45 above zero. A big Chinook wind came in as it usually does once in the winter and the little snow we had was diminishing very fast.

I want to pause here and just talk a little about TB. Most of you readers that live in the Lower 48 don't even hear about TB anymore, but it continues to haunt our Alaskan villages. Every year we have pocket epidemics. When I started Public Health nursing in Nome in 1991 we were TB testing all students every year. This continued until about 2013 when we stopped doing every student except certain grades and new students. I continued with doing it to all the students just because you never knew when there was going to be an outbreak. We continue to have issues with drug resistant forms of TB. In the villages, sometimes it is hard to keep track of people. There are a lot that just leave the village and go to another so it requires a lot of time, patience and phone calls to track them down. It gets really hard when they go to a big community like Fairbanks or Anchorage. Maybe they don't take their meds and then that is where drug resistance comes from.

I went to Venetie that next month and it was 53 below zero. That was the morning temperature. It was scheduled to warm up to -35. Not many come to the clinic when it is that cold. School was never canceled at that temperature but sometimes parents did not send their children because they would have to walk to school since snowmobiles are hard to start at -50. When I was scheduled to leave the village after the trip was finished, I missed the first flight out. My ride forgot me. The second flight of the day was canceled due to the ice fog. As you remember from the dog stories the dog's breath can form the ice fog, well so can the smoke from the wood stoves. Also, there are temperature cut offs for the airplanes. The Navajo planes cutoff temp is -45. The Cessna Caravan turbine engine cutoff temp is -60.

Fort Yukon was on CNN that week for being the coldest place in the world at -51 as a high temperature. I heard it was -50 at home in Two Rivers.

Since I had missed the flight I spent that night sleeping in the school as usual (and as usual on the floor) and someone broke into the school. This happened at 2;30 am. He walked into the classroom I was in sleeping on the floor between desks causing the motion lights to come on. He made up an excuse as to why he was there in the school and why he wanted to speak to me. He said he left his medicines in the gym and when he could not find them there he wanted to see if I had them. I have to give him credit for thinking that fast on his feet for that excuse. I was sleeping on the floor in the second-grade room, he could not have known I was there until he walked in to look to take something. He left the classroom and I got up and looked around for him in the building and then I called the principal. The principal and his wife came over and we called the troopers. He had broken into the school several times in the previous two weeks. These have also been reported to the troopers but they have not come. Venetie did not have a trooper that lived there or a VPSO (village police safety officer). The trooper told me there were going to have to be two or more troopers to go up there for this guy because there was an officer safety warrant on him. The last time he was taken into custody he threatened to kill the next State Trooper that came up here. The principal had me spend the rest of the night locked in his office for my safety. The next morning, I went to get all of my supply bags that were in the library and found that the guy had been in them and had also stolen money and my checkbook. Interestingly enough a trooper met my plane back in Fairbanks to interview me about the break in. In the State troopers defense, Alaska is an extremely large state and there are never enough troopers to cover it all so they have to prioritize what they respond to. Homicides come before breaking and entering.

That February, I had a trip scheduled to Fort Yukon. A man from Fort Yukon died in Venetie the week before. I flew into Fort Yukon but knew that the day was not going to be productive at the clinic. The funeral for the man was the same day. The clinic closed at noon except for emergencies, the school shut down for the funeral. It was amazing at the time how the whole village stopped for the funeral. I went to the funeral. The viewing was from noon until 1:00pm. The body was lying in a beautifully handmade coffin. One of the girls at the clinic lined it in purple material. The body was not embalmed as is the custom here. There was also no vault in the ground to put the coffin in. Before the actual service started at 1:00 pm, the top of the coffin was screwed on. This was just a little disturbing, but I guess not as bad as it would have been 50 years ago with a hammer and nails. There was no music playing, all you heard was the screw gun. After the funeral the coffin was taken to the cemetery in a truck. People followed on foot and in vehicles from the church to the cemetery. Now you might be thinking how were they going to bury him in ground that has been frozen all winter? The digging starts as soon as the person dies. A fire has to be built to thaw the ground. It takes a while for the ground to unfreeze enough to be dug with a shovel. There are a lot of men who usually participate in digging the grave. They dig until they reach frozen ground again, build another fire and thaw more ground. This can go on for three days depending on how long it takes to unfreeze enough ground. The coffin was lowered into the ground and men with shovels began to throw dirt on the coffin. The people gathered at the cemetery began to sing hymns and read scriptures. This was done until the grave was filled and the homemade cross set in the ground. The coffin and the cross are made by hand. There is never any store-bought coffin and rarely a granite stone. There are a few headstones that families have paid for and of course if the deceased is a veteran they get a veteran headstone. Usually there is a wooden cross that has been made and carved with the dates and the names. The cross and the coffin are embellished a lot of times with things that represent the deceased. For instance, there might be a moose, or a fish, or a dog team and sled. The person is buried in Native clothing, men usually in a moose hide vest, beaded gloves and beaded slippers, the females dressed in beaded attire. The family then puts flowers on the grave. These flowers are mostly plastic or silk due to the cold. After this everyone goes to the community hall for the funeral potlatch. Similar to a potluck but there is so much food. The food consists usually of chicken, ham, moose, salmon, duck, macaroni and cheese, pasta salad, green salad, homemade bread and dessert and last but not least moose head soup.

If it is not hunting season the village has to ask the Alaska Department of Fish and Game if they can harvest a moose for the funeral. When you think about it, it is kind of sad. In the Interior, having a moose for potlatch food has been a tradition for a hundred or more years and you have to ask permission!!! A year from now there will be a memorial potlatch held in the deceased's honor in which the family will give gifts to those who meant something to them or were good friends of the deceased. The family will spend the next year accumulating these gifts. They range from yarn to guns to jams to beaded items. Sometimes families will wait more than a year just because of finances or because they are trying to make things for the giveaway. I have been to villages where there is a giveaway at the funeral potlatch. There are two villages in the lower middle Yukon that do a Stick dance as their memorial potlatch. At one time there were more villages in that area that did them but now only Nulato and Kaltag. I will not explain that tradition here. It is better to see it. I have not had the experience of attending but plan to do so in the near future. I have heard stories and traditions regarding the celebration. I will say, a lot of those who are no longer on the earth plane come to Stick dance.

In villages in the Interior there are subtle differences when it comes to death as well beside what was mentioned above. In all villages, no matter where the body is there is at least one person with the body the entire time until burial. Most bodies are moved to the community/Tribal hall. There is usually more room and people cook and eat in the hall while awaiting the funeral and burial.

In one village, I was there when the body of a man I knew was brought back and I stayed a few days to help with the preparation. The body was brought to the Tribal hall and around the body were chairs. At the foot of the body were two very large bowls. One was full of cigarettes and one full of candy. Hmm, I was thinking, was this symbolic for him in the afterlife or what. I found an older person to ask and they told me that the cigarettes and candy were for anyone there. People played Pan (card game) late into the night. All three meals were cooked and served for anyone who wanted to come.

Since the bodies are not embalmed it is very important to keep them iced down so people would be checking and hauling in ice.

SPRINGTIME

Winter is very long in Alaska and by the end of March the sun is gloriously bathing us with its heat for longer hours. The outside temperatures are in the upper 20s and 30s and it is carnival time in the villages.

The village carnivals have been taking place for a long time. It started as a way to get people's winter furs from a season of trapping out and sold and to visit other family and friends in other communities they did not see all winter. It was and still is a fun time. Dog races dominate the carnivals and were the main event in the old days. There are men's races, women's races, kids' races, old women's races, old men's races and Cheechako races (for someone who has never been on a dog sled before). The carnivals also have other competitions including wood chopping, tea making, shooting and other fun games for kids. There are also snow machine races.

There is food galore and in most communities there is a lot of traditional food that is served.

In 2006, I went to Venetie for a clinic trip and had fortunately timed it to coincide with spring carnival. There was a potlatch at the community hall. There was salmon and salmon eggs, caribou head, caribou tongue, caribou and moose soup and macaroni salad. I tend to gorge when there is that much good food. Even the caribou head, which was my first, was tasty. It is a delicacy. It is kind of weird though to be cutting portions of meat off of a head that is turned upside down with the lower jaw removed but the upper teeth still intact and sometimes they even have some moss still embedded in them. The head is usually cooked by roasting over a fire. There was also an elder who had boiled up an unborn caribou calf that morning. It is superstitious for anyone other than elders to eat the unborn calf. For elders it is supposed to help their bones. They boil it whole, "still on the hoof" and then just peel it and eat it. That part I have not been present for. There was a dance every night as usual during carnival and in Venetie it is mostly fiddle music.

When I first saw dancing like they do in the Upper Yukon Villages, including Venetie and Arctic, it amazed me that the elders were playing fiddles and the traditional fiddle dances they were doing were very much reminiscent of the Virginia Reel and other dances I had learned in school. But thinking about it, when the traders and miners came to Alaska they brought with them their music, dances and instruments. There is still traditional Native dancing and singing with a skin drum but in the Yukon Flats region the fiddle dances and fiddle music have also become tradition. They also jig, which is similar to clogging. The foot work is just a little different. It is interesting that if you continue down the Yukon River from Fort Yukon to Beaver and Stevens Village, it seems like there is an imaginary line drawn there in regards to fiddle music and dancing. The people in the lower middle Yukon and Lower Yukon villages do not dance to the fiddle music like they do in the Upper Middle Yukon, they play mostly rock and roll at dances. Interestingly, that area was infiltrated by traders, trappers and non-natives before places like Venetie and Arctic Village. They do fiddle music and fiddle dances and jigging in the Native villages in Yukon Territory of Canada as well. Every year in Fairbanks the Athabascan Fiddle Festival is held. Musicians come from villages all up and down the Yukon all the way to the mouth. None of them are trained musicians. They all have learned to play by ear. In the spring, the third weekend in March they hold another weekend long fiddle dance that coincides with the Open North American Sled Dog Race. It is fun to attend a fiddle dance and I highly recommend it and to learn to jig and two step.

THE BABY

It was July 5th. We (myself, doctor and diabetic nurse) were on our way to Arctic Village in the Guardian Flight Cherokee. We were abeam Fort Yukon on our way north when we got a message over the aircraft radio asking if we could stop in Fort Yukon. There was a woman in labor. We landed and got picked up. The woman was said to be 4 months pregnant. She was already in the clinic emergency room when we arrived. The doctor said she would check her and I went and got a doppler (there was no OB monitor) so I could check the fetal heart rate and tone for any decelerations. The doctor did her check and said the head was " right there" but then asked me if she should give terbutaline (a medication that stops contractions). I know we were thinking that the baby was only 4 months in utero but the head was already there, there was no stopping that baby now! I lost faith in the doctor then and asked her if she would be okay with me delivering and she could do the intubation since I was not allowed to intubate a newborn even though I was NALS (Neonatal Life Support) certified. The woman had an unknown Group B strep status so the PA that was there in the clinic decided he would go get the meds mixed to hang. Never saw him again. He had wanted nothing to do with the delivery. He had never done one. There was a PA student present and I asked her to check the fetal heart tones with the doppler. I did an in and out bladder catheterization on the woman and just as I took off my gloves to put on another pair, out pops the baby. Baby looked good; she looked a lot older than 4 months. I suctioned her, cut the cord and handed her to the doctor. I then waited to deliver the placenta. While I was waiting the doctor said, "we need to have the baby skin on skin." The mom said " No, I am not going to touch that baby." I then asked the doctor to come deliver the placenta and I went over to the other gurney and unbuttoned my pants, pulled up my shirt and the baby got laid on my belly and we continued to rub her and give her a blow by oxygen. The medivac had been called when we originally arrived but they were not able to get there until about 20 minutes after the baby was on my belly. It was very interesting that while the baby was on my belly she was inching her way up to try and nurse. Haha she would have been in for a big surprise.

I cannot tell you how much I appreciated having worked OB in Anaconda Hospital 2 years prior to this. It was not scary for me and it was like I had done it my whole life.

The interesting thing was that I got a little reprimand from my nursing director when I got back because I delivered the baby. She told me I never should have done that since there was a more experienced doctor there but I told her when the doctor asked me the terbutaline question, I thought I was the most experienced at that time.

CULTURE STORY

I was traveling to Arctic Village one August to start school screening for the fall. I found out after I scheduled the trip that there was a science camp being held for all the school students "up the mountain". By the time I arrived via bush plane all the students were on the mountain, so what I had to do was get on a four-wheeler and go up the mountain to do my TB testing.

So, on the side of the mountain overlooking the village, I lined up all the students and I did the ppds while Laurie, my clerk, did all the recording. I stayed up there the rest of the day to help out with the camp and even learned a few things, like how to tell the difference between a male and female chum salmon. I also helped one of the elders make a deadfall. A deadfall was used by the old people to catch wolverines and if set up right was a sure way to get them so they could not escape. The students seemed to enjoy the time up there but wanted to get back to the village in the late afternoon. The science camp had scheduled a big potlatch on the mountain for the last night but the children did not come back. Several of the adults and elders did and some were going to camp out up there. One of the guys my age told me that in the 70s when the village had no electricity he would look up on the mountain and see the campfires of all the elders that would go up there and spend the night. They used it as a place to camp and go out and look for caribou and to pick blueberries.

Fall time in Arctic Village is absolutely gorgeous. Think of the beautiful colors in the Northeast and the mountains of NC during the leaf changes. That is what it is like but the colors are on the ground. The willow turns yellow and the blueberry bushes turn a beautiful red color. It is breathtaking to fly around that country during that time of year.

MUSKRAT

On one of my trips to Fort Yukon, one of the women who worked in the clinic brought in two skinned and gutted muskrats and set them in the kitchen. Muskrat hunting is done in the spring when you can see the muskrat houses pushed up on lakes. Anyway, although these muskrats were missing their hands, feet, innards and tails, they were not missing their head complete with beaver-like teeth. Yes, they were going to be our lunch. One of the women washed them and put them in a pan and stuffed them with onions, carrots and sprinkled them with garlic salt. I had never tried muskrat before. When I lived in Kentucky there was a trapper who used to give me skinned muskrat for the dogs and the dogs loved them. Lunch time came and the muskrats were nice and brown and I dug in. After I took a few bites, I said to my co-workers, " that is some darn good rat". I have to admit it was very tasty, very dark sweet meat. I did forgo eating the head. Later at a potlatch in Fairbanks, I tried muskrat tail and I have to say I will never eat that again. I did have a chance in my travels to eat beaver head and really liked that.

CHAPTER 13

MORE DOG STORIES

O ne day shortly after Christmas in 2005, My neighbor, Bill, and I decided we would run dogs together. I thought maybe a 40-mile run would be good. We were due to leave at 10:30 am. I decided to leave early and do a 10-mile loop before meeting him. He lived on the trail system about a mile from my house. I had six dogs hooked up to the sled. That is all I could run with the snow conditions that day. The snub line got tangled and when I untangled it the dogs popped the snow hook and ran off without me. I still had a hold of the snub line and was dragging behind the sled working hand over hand to try and get to the overturned sled, to try and right it and set the hook but I could not, it was too much for me and I could not hold on. I ran into the house to call Bill, the guy who I was going to meet and told him the dogs were on their way to his house without me. I jumped onto my 4-wheeler and had to start it three times before I could move it. It was 0 degrees. I sped up the road sliding around the corners and saw a truck following my dogs. The driver hit the trail but was unable to drive her truck onto the trail so she started out on foot to try and catch the team. I passed her, giving her a thank you wave and sped on. On the trail I could see the dogs and up ahead and I saw Bill walking up the trail. He stopped, got in a football stance to try and catch the sled. (it is much wiser to catch the leaders). He missed the sled but he slowed them down long enough for me to catch up with the four-wheeler and get in front of them to cut them off. He ran up and stood on the brake while I strung them out again and it was then I realized he was dressed in just his long underwear and bunny boots!. He had been in the middle of dressing when I had called. I told him I was going to take the dogs on and would do the loop and meet him back at his house by the time he was ready. I took the dogs onto the trail and did the 10-mile loop and as I was about 1/4 of a mile from Bill's house I saw him stopped in the road with his team heading toward me, not the way we were planning to go. It seems that as he had just gotten his dogs hooked up they pulled the hook on him and he drug across the road. He had a terrible tangle and it took about 10 minutes for him to get his tangle undone. I could do nothing but stand on his snow hook and mine to keep the teams still. There was not enough snow here to set the snow hook and get off especially on the road. Once he got his dogs lined out they turned around on him and went running to where I had just come from. I told him I would meet him further down the trail. He went to the hayfield , made a loop and returned to follow me. The rest of the run was pretty uneventful even with the Chena Hot Springs road crossing. Our trail on the east side of Two Rivers crosses the road. The dogs did the crossing with perfection. After we crossed the road then we were on the Yukon Quest trail. There was very little snow and a lot of frozen overflow. About 6 miles from the road crossing is an old, abandoned roadhouse, complete with the barn and even furniture still in it. It appears to have had its heyday in the gold rush when roadhouses were all over the trails in Alaska and people traveled by dog team and horse. The trip was good and we made the road crossing on the way home just before it got dark, 4:00 pm. I was so sore when I got home and we had done about 50 miles that day. I did miss running all of my dogs but with that little snow running 10 dogs with a sled was just not safe. I had one dog that could pull the 4-wheeler by himself. Although the farther away from home we got on the trails the more snow there was but the problem was getting to that point. I should just have run all the dogs using a four-wheeler but it is much warmer on the sled. You are not sitting on a hunk of metal and can get off the sled and run beside it to keep warm.

HAMBURGER RUN

The Two Rivers Dog Mushers used to put on a race called the Hamburger Run. It was called the Hamburger Run because the race finished at the Angel Creek Lodge, a place known for its hamburgers. I entered the race for several years, but this story takes place in 2006. It was a passenger race. I did not have a passenger so my penalty was that I had to harness and hook up by myself. Not much of a penalty for me since I did it every day on my own. During the musher meeting the race marshal said there was going to be some overflow and some open water on the Chena River. They joked and said that overflow could be anywhere from 1 inch to five feet and believe it or not they weren't far off. The race start was a mass start (all the teams leave at the same time). No one could harness or hook up until the race marshal threw his hat in the air. It was also a poker run. So, the winner was going to be the one with the best poker hand. There were people on the trail giving out playing cards. I did not win the poker part but had a good race and a good time. About 6 miles into the race there is a blind turn that comes out by the gold rush era roadhouse. The last time I ran that way the trail was good. This time as I was running around the turn I heard a lot of dogs barking. Just as I could see what was in front of me, I slammed the snow hook into the ground. There were 4 teams in front of me wallowing through overflow. I had to wait there until the teams cleared out since there was no room to pass. By this time another team had come up behind me. I pulled the hook and off into the overflow we went. The dogs were all strung out running and swimming and I was propped up on my handlebar with my feet in the air trying not to get wet when WHAM!!! the sled lurched to a stop. It had gotten caught on a small tree trunk under the overflow. The sleds do float for the most part but there is still a little that sinks under water. So, off the sled I came. I landed in the overflow that was above my knees then had to flip the sled to get it off of the stump. While I was working at this the young musher that was behind me tried to pass me and her dogs that did not want to swim jumped onto my sled and even tried to work their way into the basket of my sled via the handlebar. I wish I had my camera. All the while my leaders were going back and forth in the overflow looking for a better trail. When her leaders caught up with mine they got into a slight tangle. She had a passenger in her sled that was getting wet. Needless to say, I then had to drag myself through the knee-high water to try and get back on the runners. When I was on the sled again we passed another team. I had worn my moose hide mukluks and they were soaked through but it was warm enough my feet did not get cold. And thank God for Carhartt overalls. They got soaked and froze but what I was wearing underneath stayed dry. We continued on passing a few more teams. Every time I got off the sled to run uphill it felt like my legs weighed 50 pounds due to the frozen overalls. We crossed some more overflow but it was more like an inch deep. About 5 miles from the finish, it was getting warmer and was a little above freezing so the snow was getting slushy. When the snow gets warm it sticks to the runners, so that and the ice that had accumulated on the sled made a lot of extra weight. About a mile from the finish, we were on the Chena River and part of it was open and rushing. Sled dogs don't like the sound of rushing water, so as soon as they heard it my leaders made a 180. I was able to hook down and take the leaders and walk them through the running water. Once the leaders got across the rest of the team was yanking to go.

We arrived at the checkpoint in good time. It was not until I was ready to load my sled onto the top of my dog box did I realize how much ice had accumulated on it. The dog mushers group did say it was going to be a fun race and that was no lie. I was the winner that year.

CHAPTER 14

FUN STUFF

One of the pilots I flew to the villages grew up in the Bush in a cabin in the Arctic National Wildlife Refuge. We became good friends and had many adventures. My first trip with him up North was in April of 2006. We were going up to help the family get caribou for the summer. His family mainly subsisted on caribou. We first landed in Fort Yukon to see part of the spring carnival. As we were flying up and were about 50 miles from the cabin, there was not one inch of ground below that was not covered by caribou tracks and it was as far as the eye could see from the air. Just miles and miles of chewed up ground from the migration to the calving grounds further North. I sure wish that I could have seen the migration go through. We did see some sporadic herds of stragglers. We unloaded the plane, gathered a rifle and camera and went out on the snow machine looking for caribou. It was not long until we found a small herd. They were so much fun to watch and such beautiful animals. My friend wanted four caribou to last the summer. We shot three. While my friend hauled the first two back I waited with the third caribou. Using it as a back cushion, I sat down in the snow and looked around at the scenery. There were marten, wolverine, caribou tracks everywhere and the silence was deafening. I had not heard that kind of silence since I lived on the homestead outside of Manley. From where I was sitting the view was stunning. We were on the eastern side of the Brooks Range where the terrain is partly tundra and partly boreal forest. The weather was perfect. It was sunny and about 20-25 degrees that day. When we were ready to haul the last caribou out I got on the snow machine behind my friend. It was an old small Elan so I was very cramped. The caribou was tied on the back dragging behind the machine. I had my rifle on my back and at one turn I fell off the machine onto my back and was hit in the head by a caribou hoof as it went by me. With the gun on my back, I had sunk partially into the snow, I felt like a turtle that had been put on its shell. My friend eventually noticed I was not there and came back to get me. We continued back to the cabin and butchered out the caribou. I skinned one and a half by myself. This was my first time doing an entire animal. As I was sitting there skinning, I thought to myself, what a long way I had come from growing up in Maryland never having thought about Alaska. Here I was in the Arctic skinning a caribou knowing that all the animal was going to be used for food. The head and stink cord were going to an elder in Fairbanks. When we finished the butchering we went back to the warm cabin and ate PB&J while listening to the radio. The cabin was small and that family had raised 3 of their 5 children in that cabin. It was very cozy once it was warm. It was made out of log by hand and. only had two rooms. The entry door into the cabin was low and the ceilings were just about 6 ft high. This is to more efficiently heat it. The warm wood stove heat really had nowhere to go except to warm the cabin. In higher ceiling places the warm air would rise and stay in the ceiling. If you look at most old Bush cabins, none of them had very tall ceilings for this reason. But you could keep cold things on the floor by the walls, and you always had to wear slippers. The outhouse was three sided as most are in the Bush., so you can watch the scenery while sitting there. It was made of log and over time the logs had shrunk so you had to make sure as a woman that your aim was right into the hole or you would get wet pants. You had to back in because there was not enough room to walk in and turn around.

The morning after was gorgeous. My friend left with the snow machine to pick up a toboggan that had been left in the woods. This would be better for me to ride on instead of on the back of the little Elan. While he was doing that I pulled a chair outside and sat in the sun. It was warm enough for just a polar fleece and Carhartt bib overalls. We did get one more caribou. When we returned we went ice fishing in the lake for pike. We only got one pike. We threw it back and did not catch another. The family has two cabins one on a lake and one 17 air miles away on the Sheenjek river. We left the lake cabin for the Sheenjik and as we were taking off you could see the pike all schooled up in the lake. On the way back and forth from the Sheenjek we saw more caribou just lounging around on the snow in the sun. Most of these caribou still hanging around were pregnant cows. They could not move as fast as the males. We spent the night there and the next morning were headed to Fairbanks. We were loaded with 4 caribou. We made it past Fort Yukon and the weather was down over the White Mountains. We turned around and went back to Fort Yukon. We stayed there until a commercial flight came in so we could talk to the pilot. We tried again after talking to the pilot and had a strong headwind but made it.

SHEEP HUNT

It was August, time for sheep hunting. The only sheep hunt I have ever been on. I flew up with my friend in his plane. The plan was to land at Grasser strip about 70 miles north of Arctic Village. We were unable to land due to the weather so we turned back south then east and landed at a place called Last Lake. The airstrip is in an old lakebed. A lake was there until the late 80s when an earthquake happened and drained the lake. The weather was closing down. The weather had been bad up there like in Fairbanks for a week according to two other hunters that we met there. There was snow down to about 2,000 feet. We were surrounded by mountains. If you have ever seen pictures of the Brooks Range this was a typical picture. The weather was cold, windy and very overcast. We set up a tent under one of the airplane wings and went to sleep.

It rained most of the night. When we awoke the next morning, the mountains were all fogged in so we went back to sleep. When we woke up later the weather had lifted a bit and we gathered backpacks and started hiking. There were small pools of water on the ground in between small tussocks on the side of the mountain. Leaning down and taking a drink rewarded my mouth with some of the best water I have ever had. No taste really, just cold and wet. There were several waterfalls, many shed caribou antlers but all in all it was very "hungry" country. We only saw a few ptarmigans and eagles. We saw bear, wolf, moose and caribou tracks but nothing live. We spent many hours hiking and glassing. Of course, sheep were not to be found because the snow hid them well. We came back to camp and slept again. I think we actually slept for 12 hours, nothing else to do but burrow down deep in the sleeping bag. Saturday came and the weather had not improved. We hiked around in the valley, fished for grayling and did some berry picking. My friend decided we should turn back home because the weather showed not much sign of lifting and we did not want to get stuck there. We also feared it would start snowing and ice the plane. We flew toward the Sheenjek river to maybe stay at the family homestead and hunt caribou, but the caribou were not there yet. I was very sad that we did not stay out. I wanted to camp out for four days, which was the original plan. We did land on a gravel bar on the Porcupine river north of Fort Yukon and have supper before we continued home.

We had many more adventures including spring beaver trapping. One spring we caught quite a few and I got to skin my first one with my friends' guidance. I think the elders would have laughed at my attempt. I left so much fat on the hide and very little on the beaver. Beaver is good, especially smoked and then barbecued.

MOOSE

Several years later, I was able to do my first moose hunt. I went with my current partner, Jim, to his moose camp. It was a wall tent set on a little hill on a lake. We flew in, flew around looking for moose. You can't fly in and shoot, you have to fly in and spend the night before you can start hunting. So, we set up camp and by dark we were eating supper. The wall tent had a nice Yukon stove in it and fortunately Jim could reach it from his cot to fill it up in the morning so I did not have to get up until it was toasty warm. We were sleeping on cots with caribou hide on them and then snuggled into a sleeping bag. The caribou hide provided a lot of warmth. For many in Alaska who camp out in the fall and winter, a hide is indispensable. It can even be laid right on the ground and then with a sleeping bag on top, you do not get cold.

The next morning, we got up and went looking for moose. We walked around the lake and heard one a little ways off in the bushes. Jim did some calling and here it came. He shot it. We did not have enough time to butcher as the light was leaving, so we opened it up and tied one of the hind legs to a bush so that rigor would not prevent us from being able to spread its legs to butcher it, then we left it for the night. I worried all night that a bear or wolves were going to eat it. The next morning we boated over with the little zodiac and began to butcher. Now we had to offload out of the boat and walk through some marsh to get to the moose. I would say maybe 1/10- 2/10 of a mile off the lake. We began to butcher. It got warm that day, so warm I could take off everything on top except for my long underwear top. I still had my hip waders on as we needed them to get through the marsh. As it got warmer, little chickadees started coming in and landing on the branches of the small black spruce trees surrounding us hoping for a little bite. We would throw them small pieces as we butchered. During the middle of the butchering, we started hauling out to the zodiac. The boat was getting full and Jim decided he would boat back to camp and get the airplane, bring it back and hook it to the zodiac and it would help haul the meat back because we could not fit both of us and all of the meat in the boat. It took us about 8 hours to butcher, pack and haul the moose back to camp. It was just about dark when we got back and I was exhausted, but we still had to hang it so no animals would get it. It had been a beautiful day but it started to rain. YUCK. The meat was in game bags hanging in trees but getting a little wet.

The plan was, the next morning, to get up early and start ferrying the meat back to Fairbanks. My truck was parked at the East ramp of the airport in Fairbanks so Jim was going to take me and some meat into Fairbanks and load it in the truck and I was going to drive to the community of Nenana, which is about 45 minutes south of Fairbanks, but a closer place for him to land coming from the lake. We figured it was going to take 3 trips to get all the meat out. The weather was down that morning so we had to wait until it lifted. We took off and flew over the moose carcass, curious to see if anything, like wolves or bears had been on it overnight. We did not see anything feeding on it but we did see a wolf close to it. It got scared off by the plane but I am sure it returned after we left and the drone of the plane could not be heard. To get to Fairbanks from the lake you have to fly right over Nenana. As we started coming over we realized that the weather had gone down in Fairbanks. We listened to the weather on the radio and sure enough it was too low to land in Fairbanks. Jim made the decision to land in Nenana. We then had to decide what to do. We saw another plane land. Jim knew the pilot and he had a passenger with him who had a vehicle at the airport. I bummed a ride with him back to Fairbanks to get my truck while Jim turned around and flew back out to the lake to get the last load of meat. That moose fed us for five years.

CHAPTER 15

FLYING

I decided in February of 2007 that I wanted to learn how to fly. It was nice having a friend that flew whom I could ride with but I could only go when he wanted or wanted me to go. I began my flight lessons in a Cessna 150. It was hard for me learning how to land but once I practiced I could do it. Maybe not perfect all the time but I felt like I could at least get it on the ground. It was on that New Year's Eve that I took my check ride. It was a check ride to remember. My FAA examiner was about 80 years old. He forgot his headset so I had to borrow one from a friend of mine. He could not keep it close enough to his mouth and he did not hear well so he was having a hard time hearing the tower talking to me so he would be talking to me at the same time. He also did not see well and had a hard time seeing the instruments; therefore, he could not see what compass heading we were at or read the altimeter that was in front of him.

On my last landing at the Fairbanks Airport, he decided that my RPMs were not high enough for the cold weather and he started messing with the throttle and who knows what else, I was just trying to fly the airplane, and the engine stopped. Now you are supposed to be examined on a PRETEND engine failure, not a real one. So anyway, the engine quit, the prop stopped, I called the tower and told them we had an engine failure and we were landing NOW! I was unable to restart the plane in the air. When we landed I tried to prime the engine to restart on the ground and the primer came out in my hand. The fire engines arrived to make sure we were not on fire and we had to be towed to the parking space. The FAA examiner signed me off as we had completed the check ride and told me I had passed. YAY!! I did have to call my flight instructor and tell him about the primer, it was his airplane.

A few days later, I got a call from the FAA wanting me to come in and explain what happened. They decided after talking with the examiner and myself they were not satisfied with my getting the license. They said I had not done all the landings required even though I told them we had done the short field and soft landing at the same time. So here we go, I had to do it all over again. Now I had no airplane because the one I was using was now having to have work done so I had to find another instructor with a plane and use that one. I found one and it was a Cessna 172 as opposed to a Cessna 150. I was able to pay the owner to use it and check me out in it. I then had to schedule another examination. I passed that one also.

I decided after I got my license that what good was having the license if I did not have an airplane. I went to Anchorage with Dan, and flew a few. I went back to Fairbanks, looked at a few more, went back to Anchorage and found one. I bought a Cessna 172 straight tail, baby blue and white. My friend Dave flew it back to Fairbanks with me. I could not believe it, I had an airplane, now where was I going to go. I flew up to the Brooks Range, landed on a lake, and flew to Fort Yukon a few times.

One of the times I was on my way back from Fort Yukon, coming back to land at Bradley strip in North Pole and the engine quit. I was just over the highway when it quit. I was close enough to the strip that I did not try to restart the airplane. I figured I could make it to the strip and land. I did, I just flew it and it was a smooth landing. When I landed I looked around trying to determine why I had to " dead stick it in". I then remembered I had turned my fuel to one tank as I was supposed to do when I was flying higher than 7500. Doing that is supposed to prevent a vapor lock. Well, I did not switch to both tanks when I came down from that altitude. This taught me a valuable lesson ....ALWAYS LOOK AT YOUR CHECKLIST, no matter what you think you know or remember.

I was a little stunned and grateful that the plane did not quit farther North or I would have had to figure out where to land to miss the highway.

I flew a lot of sled dog transport with the plane and I would always fly to Tanana in the summer to catch a boat up to fish camp. Most of the summers I flew the plane to Tanana, I would have to leave it there when I left the fish camp because there always seemed to be a wildfire that prevented me from flying it home. So, a month or so later I would have to catch a bush flight to Tanana and fly the plane home. I flew friends back to villages and sometimes just flew around for fun.

I flew a lot for a while and then other things took my attention. I sold the plane in May of 2000, right after COVID started. I had not flown much in a couple of years before that and I hate to see planes just sitting on the tarmac falling apart. I was always a fair-weather flier, it had to be clear with no wind.

Unknown Eskimo girls in
Wales in 1999

Coming down 2nd
Avenue, Open
North American
Sled Dog Race

Salmon strips
hanging in the
smokehouse

CHAPTER 16

FISH CAMP

This is my place of refuge. It is the place I go in the summer to relax, and rejuvenate myself. It is also A LOT of work.

I started going to a fish camp on the Yukon River in 2009. The camp belonged to my friend Linda. The current fish camp she had for over 30 years but had been on the river since the 1970s. I went for the first time for a week, loved it so much I went the next year for two and continued going for two weeks every year until she decided she was going to stop fishing. She handed the camp over to me and I continue to go for a month to 6 weeks in the summer. The past two years we have not been allowed to fish so my time there was less but Linda and I decided that even if we are not fishing it is still the place to be in the summer. There is no running water, no electricity and no cell phone. That is why it is so wonderful. When we are fishing, we fish for King Salmon, some of the best in the world and in that part of the Yukon River, I think it is the best fish, not too oily and not too dry. We fish with a set net in an eddy about 3-4 miles downriver from camp. In the old days the salmon were plentiful and a lot weighed in the 50–60-pound range. Now, or at least the last time we fished they were only in the teens to 20-pound range and not as plentiful. This has been for a variety of reasons that I won't discuss here as it is the subject of a whole book and a lot of debate.

Opening up camp and closing it down can take a couple of days. When we open camp we have to move the fish boxes to the other side of the river. These are wooden boxes that we run cold water from a creek into to keep the salmon cold until we are ready to filet them. We have to roll the heavy boxes from camp, which is on a hill, down the hill into the boat and then get the hard plastic water hose out of the trees down the bank, tied to the side of the boat. We tie it up in the trees to keep the animals from chewing on it. We also load the cutting tables into the boat. We filet on the other side of the river hoping to keep the bears away from the camp. Once we off load the stuff on the other side of the river, we then walk the plastic water hose up the creek bed until we find a suitable place to sink it in the water so it will flow down and fill the fish box. The very, very cold creek water actually gets the fish very cold. It is easier to cut a very cold fish than a warm floppy one. Sometimes the weather at camp can be warm and we are working in shorts and Xtra tuffs or sometimes it is very cold, rainy and windy and we are dressed in polar fleece, sweats and rain gear.

Camp is a small wood frame cabin with no insulation but does have a wood stove. We have a sauna, heated with wood, a three-tier smokehouse and a NEW outhouse. It is in the woods but we have to cut the grass. Cutting grass is one of those first things we do as well, because it is usually tall when we arrive at camp and mosquitos love tall grass. We haul everything up the bank to the camp by hand. We finally have a small water pump so we can pump river water up the bank for dishes and bathing and we can pump clear water in buckets from the creek on the other side of the river and then we pump it up the bank into a couple of small holding tanks for drinking and cooking. The river water is not nice to drink as it is a glacier fed river and so is filled with silt. You could drink it if you had to.

There used to be fish camps all over the river but there are very few now. Most people have stopped fishing. The elders have died and a lot of the young people don't want to do the hard work and some have to work regular jobs so can't take off for fishing. It is a dying way of life but it is a fantastic way of life.

I have an 18 ft Lowe with a blue bimini top for a fishing boat. It is a little small when you are pulling in a net with two or three people in the boat. There have been many adventure stories fishing on the River and I am sure there will be many more. I will only relay a few here.

One summer when I was at camp by myself I went to check the net. I had only 5 fish in the net. I pulled them, put them in the tub in the boat and went to push off. I pushed off and tried to lower the motor, no go, so I manually put it down. Then I went to start the motor and nothing happened. I was away from shore, so I had to grab a paddle and get myself back in the eddy so I could be pushed to shore. Once on shore again, I tried the motor, nothing, I checked the battery, it was connected. I thought well I could pull start, so I pulled the motor cowling so I could try and pull start. Nope, pull rope not there. I sat there for a while. I then decided the only thing to do was to get to the nearest camp and have someone help me. The nearest camp on that side of the river is about 3-4 miles upstream. I had a satellite phone with me but Jim had just left in the airplane headed home and no one at the camp left their sat phone on. I took the fish out of the tub, got a rope and strung them through the gills and put them in the water. I heard a boat coming, maybe I can wave them down, I thought. Ugh, they were coming down the other side of the river and most of the time when it is sunny you can't see what is happening on the other side, so they did not see me and I did not have my flare gun. I decided I should walk upriver. I had no idea how long it was going to take because parts of the bank were boulders and rocks that had to be climbed over and some was sucking clay that had to be negotiated and there was also a large creek I had to cross. I was in my Xtra tuffs (mud boots), which made it a little harder going. I got to the large creek and thankfully it was a year when the water was extremely low and I could cross easily. Most of the time it would be dangerous to cross. The only issue was the clay mud on the down river side of the creek sucked in my boots. One of my boots got really stuck so I had to get on my knees and grab a rock to hoist my boot out of the muck. As I was doing that I saw nice large black bear prints in the muck. YIKES…. I had not thought to grab my .44 that was in the boat. I made it up to the next camp and just sat at their house not saying anything, just drinking and drinking water. I finally explained my situation and they drove me back down. Charlie looked at my boat and decided that the battery terminals, even though attached, were wet underneath causing the connection not to be made. He cleaned that up for me and the motor turned over right away. I had another issue with the motor that summer within the same week and had to call on Russ, who has a camp across from me to figure it out. It is really nice having the fishing community we have because everyone helps everyone else out.

There have been times when I have been fishing by myself and checking the net and in the earlier years I have had several over 30 # fish in the net that were still alive. Trying to pull in the net by myself can be hard. One time I was trying to pull in a 30 pounder. The fish was still alive and when I yanked up trying to get the net and fish into the boat, I fell into my fish tub. The big salmon was flopping in my arms. I was holding on with all of my might because I have had fish flopping so hard in the boat they flop themselves right out of it, I did not want to lose this one.

Linda and I were out together one summer. The camp across the river from us was having bear issues. Bears love fish, bears love blueberries. Well, that year, there were no blueberries. So, the bears started coming into camps. One had been shot at the camp across the river. This camp had a lot of children there so it was a safety hazard for that bear to be sneaking in trying to get fish. Well, there was another, it had been spotted but had not come close enough to camp. As I mentioned before we kept our fish in the cold box on the other side of the river. We were getting ready to go across to do some fileting and we saw some movement on the cliff by the box. Linda grabbed the binoculars and sure enough it was a black bear. We got in the boat and were able to see the black bear snooping around our boxes. Linda had a 30.06, she was driving the boat, so I picked up the rifle and aimed to shoot. I saw that shot bounce off the rocks on the cliff. The bear moved up the cliff, startled by the shot. I aimed again and missed. The bear ran the rest of the way up the cliff and disappeared into the trees. I know I am not the best shot but I had not even taken into consideration the movement of the boat and the current. That bear did sneak into the camp across the river, with all the children, later that night and became dog food.

Weather can come on really fast on the Yukon. Linda and I had been visiting another camp not too far away and we had also set up a net by that camp a few hours before. After visiting we decided to check the net and go home. While we were checking the net we looked up and we saw a very large dark cloud rolling toward us from down river. We stopped, put our rain gear on and finished pulling the net. It started to downpour, we got the boat moving and headed toward camp.

We were only about 1/4 mile from camp, the wind came up fast, there was thunder and some lightning. The bimini top was flapping hard in the wind and got us a little scared. We pulled onto the north bank and tied off the boat and ran into the trees. Not the best place when there is lightning but better than in a boat. We stayed there until the storm passed and then we headed back to camp. One time a storm came up like that and we were in the cabin at camp and saw a person we know, who had been checking his fish wheel, boating down the river and lightning struck the water right next to him. It looked like it hit his boat. That incident is what we were thinking of when we pulled over the boat.

Time at fish camp is a time for us to visit with people we only see during that time of year. We try and have a potluck party at least once; it is hard when we are really fishing but we find at least one night we can do it and we visit for a long time. The sun never sets in the summer and we never know what time it really is. Time is only important to know when we are on a fishing schedule. Sometimes people are checking nets and fish wheels at midnight but it looks like three o'clock in the afternoon. Alaska Fish and Game regulates what days we can fish and for how long, so we do need to know what time it is for that. Time is also important to know about messages. Since there is no cell service the only way people can communicate with us is via radio messages. Family and friends call either KJNP in North Pole or KIAM in Nenana and leave messages. They are broadcast at certain times every day. This is the way it is all over the Alaskan Bush because there are many people living without phone or internet so it is a great way to communicate. Everyone huddles around the radio at the message times to hear if there are any messages for them or just to hear the Bush gossip. It is fun to listen and learn who people are from the radio but more interesting to run into those people in person and put a name to a face.

CHAPTER 17

SPRINT DOGS

I had kept distance and mid distance dogs ever since I started with dogs in 1995. It was hard to train for these types of races and travel for a living. So, I really did not race after I moved to Alaska for quite a few years. I would just participate in our local Two Rivers races. I just ran the dogs for fun. About 2012, I got to know Curtis Erhart. Actually, I had known him for a long time but got reacquainted with him since I was always visiting his father and brother in Tanana. Curtis started giving me sprint dogs that were not making his team. I was beginning to love the speed. Distance dogs when I ran the Iditarod were running about 8-10 miles an hour. Now I was running dogs that ran 18-20. It was awesome. So, I started to make the switch over. The other good thing about spring dogs is that training only takes an hour to an hour and a half a day. Not the care, but the training. I remember on one training run with the sprint dogs I ran into Rick Swenson and his team. We stopped to chat a little bit and he told me he was coming back from a 100-mile training run. I thought to myself DANG, I never did those miles on a training run even when I was training for Iditarod, but that was a different time. After we stopped talking and started back on our way, I thought to myself wow 100-mile training run. Here I left for mine after getting home from work and I will be home in time to have supper. This is my kind of training. I ran sprint dogs for 6 years, competing in the Open North American Championship (ONAC) multiple times and sometimes being the only woman. In Open class sprint racing you are allowed to run as many dogs on your team as you want. I usually only ran 16. The same I had started with in Iditarod but twice as fast and the sled is smaller and weighs less. Some of the old Open North American Race competitors would run 20-24 dogs on the line. I loved sprint racing and of course loved the dogs. I had always thought I would quit running dogs when I was 40. Then I said once I got the airplane, I would get rid of the dogs. But I did not. I so enjoyed being out on the trail.

Running the Open North American was great fun. It was the longest continuous running sled dog race in the world, until COVID hit. In March 2020 was to be the 75th year but it had to be postponed due to the epidemic. I was not running then but was the president of the Alaska Dog Mushers Association.

It takes place the third weekend in March and is at the same time as the big Tanana Chiefs Conference annual meeting. People from all of the Interior villages come in for the meeting and to see the race. It is all people talk about in the villages when you talk about dog mushing is the Open North American and Fur Rendezvous (held in Anchorage). There used to be a lot of village mushers that came in to race the ONAC. The race is live streamed on the radio and people sit in their homes in the village and listen and write down the checkpoint times. They have done that ever since the race started and some of the elders that used to have dogs have some of those old-time sheets that they made saved. It is fun to see the elders that used to race ONAC on the street and on the trail when you are the musher running the race. The ONAC is a three-day race. 20 miles, 20 miles and 30 miles.

As I said before some years I was the only woman running or one of two. I do remember one race, I was on my way to the finish line, I was in Noyes Slough. I had seen three children on my way out sledding down the bank of the slough. On my way back they had stopped and I yelled hi. I had just passed them when I heard one of the little boys exclaim , " That was a girl". I laughed all the way back.

I met some amazing people running dogs, made some great friends, saw some terrific scenery, ran and took care of some amazing athletes.

I do miss running dogs especially in the Spring when it is warmer, but I do not miss all the work it took except for training the dogs. I loved that.

One day I was splitting 300 fish, this was 7 years ago, and I thought "I am done". I love to split fish but the thought of cooking dog food at -40 and making sure I could get someone to feed dogs while I traveled was not so fun. I thought no more, no matter how much I loved the training. I really never liked racing, I just did it to give the dogs experience. I had been able to run them to Tanana for work, I had raced dogs in 10 states and Canada, I had seen scenery not many others ever had, but I was finished. I ran that winter and then sold or gave away my dogs, all but two, to other mushers or junior mushers. I kept two leaders, one of which has passed and the other who lays by my feet as I write this is very short on time.

I sit here sometimes and wonder how I ever had the time to do the dog mushing thing. Most of the older mushers I did distance racing with have now retired from dogs. I did spend 5 years as President of the Alaska Dog Mushers Association and met some wonderful people and I met wonderful sprint mushers. Some I had known in the distance world, but it was time to take a step back. As I look at this old leader who has not much time left, I get a teary eye because when he dies it will be like a whole big part of my life is in the past. I trained and raced sled dogs for 25 years, that is a big chunk of life. But, as I tease my musher friends, I now have money. Most dog mushers don't have much money, when you are feeding and taking care of a large kennel of dogs, but it is still bittersweet to know that one of the best and fun parts of my life will be past.

CHAPTER 18

OTHER JOBS

A fter I first moved to Fairbanks, I went to work on call with the Forensic Nursing Services at Fairbanks Memorial Hospital. I had been trained as a Sexual Assault Response Team nurse while I was in Montana but had not been able to do any work there using this training. The hospital in Fairbanks had a relatively new team and it was a great experience working with them. We did forensic exams on sexual assault and domestic violence victims and at times I was called in to do forensic photography on a questionable death. Most of the stuff happened in the middle of the night. I worked this on-call job for about 5 years and then one night, one story and one victim and I was finished. It was an awesome learning experience but I hand it to those nurses who do it on a full-time basis and have to see and hear the stories, especially when they involve children. I have to say that the death investigation part of forensics is more interesting to me.

ANTHC

I started doing some part time work with the Alaska Native Tribal Health Consortium (ANTHC) within their Domestic Violence Prevention Initiative Grant. I was able to travel all over the state teaching historical trauma, domestic violence, sexual assault to tribes. I traveled with some wonderful trainers and a traditional doctor Rita Blumenstein. I loved this job. I was very honored to teach with this group of exceptional women. For most of the time we traveled teaching, I was the only non-Native in the training group. I made some lasting friendships and learned so much. I still participate with them in the Garden of Roses camp that is held every summer. It is a weekend camp (gathering) for girls ages 9-15 that have been sexually abused. The grant has changed focus so I don't get to go around and teach but have been asked by other entities in the state to teach historical/generational trauma. It is something I am very passionate about and have actually done some teaching about historical trauma to students on the Fort Peck Reservation.

LEAVING PUBLIC HEALTH

I decided to leave public health after 10 years. I felt I had become stale. I also felt like the state was tying our hands in some ways and I wanted a change. I went to work for the Council of Athabascan Tribal Governments (CATG). They are based in Fort Yukon. They hired me to be the Diabetes

Educator and the Community Health Aide Supervisor. I enjoyed the job for a while, as it allowed me to work from home. I still traveled to the villages in the Fort Yukon subregion, so I knew all the people. That was the fun part. The administration part was not fun and certainly not my forte.

I learned a lot in the diabetes department and really enjoyed working with my patients, and the Community Health Aides. There was a lot I did not like about the job. I stayed with it for 4 years. I felt like more could be done but there were roadblocks always to making things better and I got very frustrated.

CHAPTER 19

THE LATEST CHAPTER

I was venting my frustration to a woman about my job at CATG. She worked in the diabetes program for Alaska Native Tribal Health Consortium. She lives in Bozeman Montana but comes to Anchorage to work on and off. She told me she knew of someone on the Fort Peck Indian Reservation in NE Montana that was always looking for nurses. She gave me his name. I called him, we talked over the phone and he invited me for a site visit. I had lived in Montana before and knew about this area. It was not the Rocky Mountain part of the state where I had lived before, it was the Great Plains. Flat but beautiful Big Sky, the reason Montana has that nickname, Big Sky Country. I liked the reservation and I really liked the Director of the Health Promotion Disease Prevention Department (HPDP). I came back home and told him I would like to work for him on 2 weeks on 2 weeks off schedule. He hooked me up with the assistant director who told me what I needed to do, fingerprints, RFP etc. I had just sent all that in and BAM, COVID hit. Good thing I had not given notice to CATG that I was leaving. I had just renegotiated my contract with them. Well, I still got to work from home and also did not have to travel. It was the only time in 15 years that I was home for 5 months in a row. It was awesome. In June of that year, I just happened to look at the Fort Peck Tribes Facebook page and there was a notice from the Chairman of the Tribe that the Tribe was going to reopen business and that all employees were going back to work 50%. I contacted the HPDP director and told him I was still interested in working and he said they would get the contract out to me and I could start. I decided to start that August, so here I was traveling two weeks a month while others were still at home. It was great, the airplane middle seats were always empty, the Seattle airport was a ghost town. Too bad it is still not like that.

It has been different working on the Rez. It is evident that Alaska Natives are more subsistent than the Reservation Natives. The rates of chronic disease are much higher I think on the Reservation. Access to healthy food is not that great, there are stores and it is on a road system but fresh fruits and veggies are expensive. Sometimes the prices rival those in Alaska. I have seen a few gardens around and HPDP has put greenhouses at most of the schools but they are not yet totally functional year-round.

It has been a great cultural experience. It is all new. There is not a lot that is the same as in Alaska, Death is done differently, celebrations are different. There are Inipi and Sun Dance, neither of which is in AK. I have been invited to Inipi and go one or more times each time I am there. I have met some amazing people and have been able to participate in some cultural things and have learned a lot about a different culture.

I was given an Assiniboine name by a friend, which was a great honor.

I have been put out on the Plains to fast overnight by myself. That was a deeply personal experience. I would love to tell you what happened but it is personal. I will say that while I was out there in the dark and wind, I heard coyotes calling all around me, I got to see the stars move throughout the night and I saw some of the old ones.

I know those who put me out there that night were a little worried I might be too cold....they did not know my dog mushing cold stories. They were worried I might be a little scared.....they did not know my stories.

My Assiniboine friends have taken me to sacred places, have shared stories, have fed me and made me a ribbon skirt for Inipi, they have shared themselves and their culture and continue to do so every time I go. This adventure is not at its end yet and I hope it does not end soon, as there is so much to learn.

I cannot say enough how all of these things that have happened to me have impacted my life. How all the people I have met through all my adventures have impacted my life.

WESTERN ALLOPATHIC MEDICINE IS NOT ALL THERE IS

During all of my experiences I have learned other ways to help people. After having studied and practiced Western medicine for so many years. I was introduced to alternative medicine, first by Phyllis D. Light in a foot reflexology class. I had gone to Alabama for a vacation and a friend of mine Amy told me I should stop and see Phyllis if I was in the area. Phyllis is a well-known herbalist and teacher. I did meet her and she told me she was holding a foot reflexology class that weekend, so I attended. I was working on her and she asked me if I had ever done any energy work. When I said no she told me I should.

A couple of years later I attended the American Holistic Nurses Association Conference. They had a session about Healing Touch. I thought I wanted to do that so I began studying energy medicine and other modalities that have been used by practitioners for thousands of years. I am now a Healing Touch Certified Practitioner, a Reiki Master, and a Cranio Sacral therapist. I am a sound healer, and also do fire cupping and Tui Na. It seems like I cannot get enough of learning. I thought after I got out of nursing school I would never go back to school. But I did but only after being out of school for over 30 years.

Besides doing all of the above I got a certificate in Integrative Health and Lifestyle from the University of Arizona and a certificate in Ethnobotany from the University of Alaska Fairbanks.

I have my own alternative medicine business and have a small client base at home in Alaska and on the Reservation that I work with and it is very rewarding to me. I would solely like to do this kind of work.

I have also become a student of the plants and have worked with some wonderful herbalists in learning about medicinal uses of plants. I have studied with Indigenous and non-Indigenous plant healers and try to learn any information I can.

I also make my own remedies which I use and give away or sell.

I continue to learn as much as I can in what is left of my life, which I hope will be long because there is so much more to learn.

CHAPTER 20

LESSONS I HAVE LEARNED

1. You are where you are supposed to be when you are supposed to be.

Having read this book I am sure that is obvious that I never thought I would end up living in Alaska or working in Indian country.

2. EVERYONE has some generational/historical trauma

I never had thought about this. I didn't even know what this meant until I was in Alaska for eight years this last time. I was traveling around teaching Domestic Violence Sexual Assault in the rural areas and came face to face with it. I began doing a lot of reading, research and listening and realized how much of this was in the Alaska Native/Native American culture. I began traveling all over Alaska teaching this and became aware from a lot of Natives that they did not know their history and did not know how much that affected them at present. As I was doing this I began thinking about my own culture and history and found that it was pervasive in my own culture. There is a reason we were Italian and not Catholic, There is a reason my father was adamant my children would never be raised Catholic. There was a reason the other side of my family immigrated after the Clearances began in Scotland. There is a reason we have our own personal trauma and community trauma. It all revolves around power and control. Every nation has had some kind of historical trauma and we still perpetuate that among each other and with our own cultures today.

3. You cannot save everyone.

I learned this lesson a long time ago in my career. Even before I started working in Indian country I found out that I could not save all of my patients. You cannot make anyone do what they need to do or what you think they should do. It has to be each person's decision whether they want to become healthy. There have been many nurses and other health professionals I have worked with in my career that think they can change their patient. Thinking they can make their patient be compliant with their diabetes diet, their exercise regimen etc. I have seen those nurses get very frustrated, they burn out very fast and start having their own health issues. You cannot make someone stop drinking or doing drugs either. It has to be their choice.

This is extremely hard to remember in Indian Country. The problems are pervasive. The alcohol, drugs, diabetes, heart problems, abuse, and neglect are rampant. It is hard to see all of the problems and not get overwhelmed. I think this is really hard for nurses to decide what to do.

I had mentioned this to an Eskimo friend once. He reminded me of the story of the little girl and her grandfather walking along the beach. There were starfish washed up everywhere on the beach. The little girl bent down and started throwing starfish back into the sea. The grandfather said what are you doing you can't save them all and she said, "If I could just save one." I have had to remind myself of that often while working in Indian country.

4. Working in Indian Country is not for the faint of heart.

You will see more sad things than you want or could ever imagine. You will find out that there are children that are physically and sexually abused and neglected on a daily basis. You will find children that only get to eat when they are in school. I just recently had a conversation with an 18-year-old that is in her senior year. The young girl said to me she does not even get birthday presents. How sad. Didn't most of us grow up with our birthdays celebrated with favorite meals, cake and presents. It just made me sad.

When working in Indian Country there is a lot of suicide, overdose, alcohol poisoning, homicide, children that are neglected, abused, stolen. But what a great and rewarding job it can be to work in Indian country.

5. Time is not as relevant as the outside world makes it.

I have mentioned this before. Of course, you may need to get to work on time. Sometimes in rural Indian country that is not a priority either. A lot of times the chronic lateness to work has no consequence.

How much does this matter to you? I think a lot of us grew up living by a clock, taught over and over again not to be late. How much of this did we put on ourselves? Could we learn a lesson from this?

6. Family is everything

Family in Indian country is very extensive. You go to your great, great uncle's funeral. You have non biological family members that ARE family and they are called aunts, uncles, sisters, sister aunts and you do anything for them.

7. Small town issues are not only in small towns

In the villages and on the Reservations there are a lot of the same problems one would find in any small non-Native town. This family does not like that family, a lot of jealousy over who bought a new snow machine or 4-wheeler, a lot of nit-picky mean talk about each other.

BUT.. different in Native communities than in non-Native communities, if there is a tragedy, such as someone dying or missing, it does not matter what family you are from everyone gathers to help cook, search, make coffins, line coffins, dig graves. Also, when it is celebration time such as fiddle dancing, spring carnival all gather for the festivities leaving aside the sometimes-cruel gossip.

8. Natives love to tease.

If they make fun of you, you are accepted. The common phrase " I joke" is said often. I would worry if no one made fun of me.

9. Natives are very giving.

I think more so than any other culture I have worked with. Other cultures are very food oriented, like Italians, Mexicans. You are to eat when offered food or it is an insult. In a lot of Alaskan Native communities, it is that way. They always have coffee or tea and if they have it they will lay out dry meat or dry fish/strips. Different from other cultures, I have found that if you need something Natives will give it to you regardless of if they can afford it or afford to even give it. If you were cold and needed mittens they would give you the only pair they have.

10. If you participate in cultural activities you are more accepted.

In the earlier part of this book, I mentioned how when working in the Norton Sound region I did not participate in much but when I worked in the Athabascan communities you could always find me at a potlatch, fiddle dance, spring carnival. In the Assiniboine/Sioux communities I attend inipi, four days, etc. It shows everyone that you appreciate their culture and want to learn more.

If you are a dog musher in Alaska you are held in a high status but if you are an Open North American or Fur Rondy veteran you really have some street cred within the Athabascan communities. It is so fun just to be recognized in the village by the elders and they always want to talk with you about dogs, what you feed, how you train and how they used to run and train dogs.

11. If you are kind it will always come back to you

In our world we have lost a lot of kindness for our fellow humans. In Indian country so many outsiders come in with their preconceived ideas about how people should be and if you are not like that then they will be angry with you.

I also know that seeing the amount of distress, and other social issues in Indian Country can be very stressful, even unconsciously to people, everyone still deserves kindness. Is it going to kill you to smile at all the people whom you work with or say hi to all the students you pass in the hallway at school. I have noticed I get a lot more respect from people and from students when I don't bring my own issues to work. If you keep saying hi to children and even adults you will begin to get the same back, it may take some time but it will happen. It also makes that person feel wanted and maybe they have so much gone on in their life they don't feel that way until you make them feel like it.

I have seen that in many of my fellow nurses that come and work in Indian country. If the person does not meet their preconceived notion or if the community as a whole does not meet their standards they are not nice.

12. Wear your cultural thinking cap

Every time I step foot into Indian Country or I go to work, I have to leave my culture at home. I have to think in another culture. I have to behave in a cultural way. A good example of this is my Italian culture is loud and talks over each other. That really does not fit well within the Native culture. I had to learn especially in the Native culture in Alaska that silence is okay. You do not have to fill up every moment with words. Alaska Natives may take a while to answer a question. Believe me, 10 seconds of silence sometimes feels like 5 minutes. There are times I have to pinch myself to keep quiet while waiting for an answer. If it is an elder it could be longer and there could be a story attached to the answer, that might take 15-20 minutes.

But just think of the wonder you could experience listening to that story or the knowledge you could get from that story.

I was asked by a health professional at a training on generational trauma if I could sum up what they needed to know about dealing with Native patients in one sentence.

I replied, "Just listen".

13. Food Insecurity

Did you know that even in Alaska and the Lower 48 states, there are Native communities with very little food or services available?

Most people would think that Appalachia may still be that way, but in many respects it has more than most Native communities.

Alaska is closer to Russia than to the Lower 48. That was very surprising to a lot of my students on the Rez. We get our store food by barge or truck. If the barge breaks down or we have severe blizzards we can have a food shortage in the stores. There are Native communities in the contiguous United States that do not have grocery stores. There are Native communities in the lower 48 that have to travel 300 miles to get to a hospital. There are Native communities still without running water/ flush toilets in both Alaska and the Lower 48.

14. The politics in Indian country can really suck.

The politics and the political climate in small villages or large Reservations is about the same. A lot has been done that has a political motive to it. Much like our government. The small mindedness also prevails, the jealousy prevails. The feeling of power prevails. To build a wellness center should not take 16 years but it does if I don't like you or your family or I think you are getting something more than me. I have thought long and hard about this because it is prevalent in all of Indian country where I have worked. It makes things so slow in getting done. I have concluded, and some of you may not like my rationale, but it seems like reverse colonization. A learned behavior from being oppressed. If you think about it in history there have been times when the conquered have become the conquerors and we have witnessed it when it is a country's own people trying to conquer them.

15. There are NOT a lot of people in Indian country that try to keep up with the Joneses.

I will give you an example. Two of my family members came to visit me in Alaska. I decided I would take them to see a village so we flew up to Arctic Village. One of them did think the area was pretty but was very taken back by the living conditions. We went to a friend's house for lunch, where we ate roasted duck. After we left, a family member said, I can't believe they live like that. I said what do you mean? She went on, they just have a plywood floor and it looks like the couch is falling apart. I had to remind my family member that housing, furniture, yards were not the priority and certainly not the measurement of the people like they thought it should be. I wonder what they would think of my friend who has 20 people living in her house, 15 of them children and they sleep on mattresses on the living room, porch, kitchen etc. Some who would see that may think this is awful but they don't know the backstory that all those children my friend has taken in so they won't be in the system or have to live in a horrible situation.

Jobs are not plentiful especially in the Alaskan villages and in a lot of Indian country money is not plentiful so they have to decide what is more important, nice furniture or food on the table.

16. Western Medicine is not all there is.

Throughout centuries many other forms of healing worked. It is time to bring them back. It is time to bring cultural healing back. Plants work, energy medicine works, prayers in the Inipi work. Medical professionals need to know that there is more to life and healing than the British Medical system under which we were all taught.

Healing too needs to be culturally appropriate.

CONCLUSION

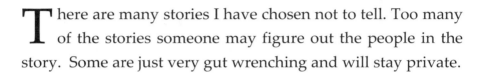

T here are many stories I have chosen not to tell. Too many of the stories someone may figure out the people in the story. Some are just very gut wrenching and will stay private.

I have related this story so that maybe I could have an influence on health professionals considering a career within tribal communities. It has been distressing and stressful at times but most of all has been more rewarding than this book could ever tell you. The rewards for me have been the places I have lived, people I have met, friendships I have made, the cultural things I have learned and been able to participate in, the medical things I have been able to see and do that I could not do anywhere else. I hope I can get at least "one starfish" to consider working, experiencing the culture before it dies out and trying to make a difference in Indian country.

I hope some of you readers, especially nurses who have thought about maybe going to Indian country to work, do it and have the same experiences I have and have the impact on your life that it has had on mine.

ABOUT THE AUTHOR

Paula Ciniero

Paula Ciniero RN, HTCP, CST-P, has been nurse for 40 years. As a graduate of the University of Maryland, she left that state after nursing school and began moving around the country making her way to Alaska. She has worked in most aspects of nursing and loves working in tribal communities. She currently practices holistic and complementary medicine, including energy medicine, cranio sacral therapy, sound healing and herbalism. When she is not traveling around the world learning indigenous healing techniques, she splits her time between Alaska and Florida. As the fish wheel turns is her first book.

Made in United States
Cleveland, OH
07 January 2025

13192504R00090